BEYOND PAST LIVES

ALSO BY MIRA KELLEY

Healing Through Past-Life Regression . . . and Beyond (2-CD set)

○

Hay House Titles of Related Interest

THE BIOLOGY OF BELIEF: Unleashing the Power of Consciousness, Matter & Miracles, by Bruce H. Lipton, Ph.D.

BREAKING THE HABIT OF BEING YOURSELF: How to Lose Your Mind and Create a New One, by Dr. Joe Dispenza

THE DIVINE MATRIX: Bridging Time, Space, Miracles, and Belief, by Gregg Braden

DYING TO BE ME: My Journey from Cancer, to Near Death, to True Healing, by Anita Moorjani

MIRRORS OF TIME: Using Regression for Physical, Emotional, and Spiritual Healing (book-with-CD), by Brian L. Weiss, M.D.

THE TAPPING SOLUTION: A Revolutionary System for Stress-Free Living, by Nick Ortner

WISHES FULFILLED: Mastering the Art of Manifesting, by Dr. Wayne W. Dyer

YOU CAN HEAL YOUR LIFE, by Louise Hay

All of the above are available at your local bookstore
or may be ordered by visiting:

Hay House USA: www.hayhouse.com®
Hay House Australia: www.hayhouse.com.au
Hay House UK: www.hayhouse.co.uk
Hay House South Africa: www.hayhouse.co.za
Hay House India: www.hayhouse.co.in

○

BEYOND PAST LIVES

WHAT PARALLEL REALITIES CAN TEACH US ABOUT
RELATIONSHIPS, HEALING, AND TRANSFORMATION

MIRA KELLEY

HAY HOUSE, INC.
Carlsbad, California • New York City
London • Sydney • Johannesburg
Vancouver • Hong Kong • New Delhi

Published and distributed in the United States by: Hay House, Inc.: www.hay house.com® • *Published and distributed in Australia by:* Hay House Australia Pty. Ltd.: www.hayhouse.com.au • *Published and distributed in the United Kingdom by:* Hay House UK, Ltd.: www.hayhouse.co.uk • *Published and distributed in the Republic of South Africa by:* Hay House SA (Pty), Ltd.: www.hayhouse.co.za • *Distributed in Canada by:* Raincoast Books: www.raincoast.com • *Published in India by:* Hay House Publishers India: www.hayhouse.co.in

Cover design: Amy Rose Grigoriou • *Interior design:* Nick C. Welch

Library of Congress Cataloging-in-Publication Data

Kelley, Mira, author.
 Beyond past lives : what parallel realities can teach us about relationships, healing, and transformation / Mira Kelley.
     pages cm
  ISBN 978-1-4019-4604-3 (hardcover : alk. paper) 1. Reincarnation therapy. 2. Regression (Psychology) I. Title.
  RC489.R43K45 2014
  615.8'528--dc23
                              2013046578

Hardcover ISBN: 978-1-4019-4604-3

10 9 8 7 6 5 4 3 2 1

1st edition, July 2014

Printed in the United States of America

To my mother, Liliana Angelova Paslieva.
Your unconditional love and support for me
mirrors the unconditional love and support
that Source has for each one of us.
Thank you! I love you!

CONTENTS

FOREWORD

Several years ago I wrote a book titled *10 Secrets for Success and Inner Peace*. The very first principle is "Have a mind that is open to everything and attached to nothing," and I cannot emphasize enough how important this has been in my own life. I have long believed that being open causes miraculous occurrences to become the norm. The benevolent forces of the universe begin to come to our aid, and Divine synchronicity "moves the pieces around," showing the ego who's really in charge.

My wife and I always raised our children to have open minds as well, and we encouraged discussion on any number of topics, including reincarnation and past-life recollections. However, although I had read *Many Lives, Many Masters* by my good friend Brian Weiss, and shared stages with him all over the world, I seldom had any firsthand experience with past-life regression. Then I met Mira Kelley.

Mira, who had worked with Dr. Weiss, contacted me a few years ago with the invitation to participate in a regression with her. She said that she intuitively felt I would benefit from the session, and wanted nothing from me other than to offer me this opportunity. I was so intrigued by her heartfelt letter that I decided to take her up on her offer.

When I called Mira about setting up a time to do the regression, she suddenly told me about a woman named Anita Moorjani, who had written an incredible description of the near-death experience (NDE) she'd experienced. Mira sent me what Anita had written, and it moved me to the point that I gave away numerous copies of it and ultimately encouraged Hay House to publish a book by this amazing woman. Anita and I became close friends, and her book, *Dying to Be Me*, went on to become a bestseller and inspire countless people. And Mira Kelley's decision to send Anita's NDE report to me sparked this stupendous chain of events.

Some time passed after I met Mira, during which we had several more conversations. Finally, she came out to see me in Maui for the regression. I had no expectations for our session, but within an hour of her arrival, I entered into one of the most riveting experiences of hypnotic time traveling imaginable. Mira recorded the entire session and transcribed every word, some of which I reproduced in my book *Wishes Fulfilled* (and Mira touches on here in *Beyond Past Lives*).

While I had almost no memory of precisely what I said during our session, the visual images were crystal clear. I am still very intrigued by all that transpired while I was in that semihypnotic state with Mira—and by all of the synchronistic occurrences that followed after meeting her. It was just another example of what happens when we keep a mind that is open to everything and attached to nothing. As one of my favorite quotes by Mark Twain reminds us, "It ain't so much the things we don't know that get us into trouble. It's the things we know that just ain't so."

I know you will enjoy this book and the insights Mira presents herein as much as I have.

—I AM,
Wayne W. Dyer

A NEW BEGINNING

I want to begin this book with an old Bulgarian ritual. This is something my beloved mother, Liliana Paslieva, and I have done on numerous occasions when I have been on the verge of a new beginning:

My mother takes a vessel of water and puts a few fresh flowers in it. She holds it in her hands and, closing her eyes, infuses the water with her motherly love. She prays that I will be protected and guided in my journey.

My mother and I stand just inside the entryway of our home. She opens the front door, pours the water on the ground, and says, "God ahead of you, and you follow."

I cross the threshold, filled with the exhilaration of a new beginning. I place one foot in the puddle on the ground and say, "God ahead of me, and I follow."

I take this first step knowing that I am ready. I leap with faith into the unknown. The crossing of the threshold symbolizes how I am stepping into my greater being—physically, emotionally, and spiritually.

I place my other foot in the puddle of water. Once again I say, "God ahead of me, and I follow."

I feel the stability and assuredness present in my feet. I am now firmly rooted on my path—the path of serving the expansion of humanity by sharing what has been revealed to me through my work.

I embark on this voyage with trust. I know I will be guided. I know that every step of the way, whatever I need will arrive to support my journey. I am grateful for all the gifts and opportunities that I already know will present themselves to me. I am grateful for the ways the information I'm sharing in this book has already changed my life. I know it will impact others' lives, too, and that it will assist them in creating a life of miracles and expansion.

So let's step across the threshold together, shall we? Join me on an adventure into past-life regression, time, transformation, and healing.

God ahead of us, and we follow.

PREFACE

My Path to Healing and
Growth Through Regression

I was 13 years old when I regressed myself for the first time. I had just read Brian Weiss's book *Through Time Into Healing* and was fascinated by the way his clients were able to resolve complicated issues after they saw their present-day challenges played out in past lives. I had no preconceived beliefs about reincarnation because I grew up in Communist Bulgaria, so religion and spirituality were not topics that were discussed during my childhood. However, the possibilities intrigued me, so I followed the instructions in the book to try a past-life regression for myself. In that first regression, I relived a life as a Soviet spy during World War II. (I tell the full story of this life in Chapter 3.) The experience was very vivid and emotional, and it greatly affected my formative years.

My life continued in much the same way as any child's. I then went to college and to law school, and I was working as an attorney in New York City when regression once again touched my life. After suffering through more than a year of debilitating pain with no relief from any of the medical professionals I'd consulted, I suddenly remembered the regression I'd done as a child. Out of desperation I called a local practitioner, and I experienced a spontaneous healing after only two sessions. The pain never returned.

At that point it became my greatest joy to share my story and the incredible possibilities offered by past-life regression. The study of it became my passion. I began attending lectures and reading every book I could find on past-life regression and reincarnation. I told my friends about all that I had learned. I knew regression worked, so for every issue that came up my suggestion was always the same: "Let's heal it through a session." I regressed all my loved ones who would agree to try it, most frequently my beloved partner.

It didn't matter that I hadn't been taught how to regress others; it felt comfortable and easy, like I had an innate understanding of how to do it. However, the next logical step on my path seemed to be taking classes, so I studied with some of the most prominent practitioners in the field: Dr. Brian Weiss and Dolores Cannon. Eventually I started my own practice and began seeing clients on weekends. The turning point was when I had the opportunity to do a regression with Dr. Wayne W. Dyer: That experience opened doors so that I have been able to fully dedicate myself to helping people improve their current lives by experiencing their past lives.

When I work with clients, they transform right before my very eyes. Their lives are never the same after the work we do together, and this gives me a tremendous sense of fulfillment and satisfaction. But the most interesting part about the work is how much I have learned about life through my clients. My greatest spiritual lessons have come to me through their explorations, and it was my desire to share these lessons that prompted me to write this book. I've deepened my understanding of things I've long heard about but had not yet internalized, and I have also discovered truths that I've never heard anywhere else before. In this way, I feel like a true adventurer exploring unknown dimensions of consciousness.

INTRODUCTION

Before we begin the book in earnest, I would like to talk about a few things to help you maximize the *Beyond Past Lives* experience. Please note the following as you read:

Chapters Are Lessons

Each of the ten chapters in this book is devoted to a lesson that has been revealed to me through past-life regression. The most basic lesson is that it *is* possible to heal your present by working with your past. I will go into more detail about this in Chapter 1, as well as explain how I guide clients through a past-life regression. In Chapter 2, I share my shocking discovery that from the viewpoint of the soul, all of our past, present, and future lives are simultaneously existing in the same "now" moment. I build on this lesson in Chapter 3 and explain how each choice we make creates a new reality. In Chapter 4, I explain the difference between your everyday "self" and your "Higher Self," and teach you how to connect with your Higher Self in any moment to receive guidance. Chapter 5 is devoted to the lesson that everything around us reflects us back to ourselves, while Chapter 6 covers the importance of forgiveness. In Chapter 7 we explore how to play with time, before going into the topic of self-healing in Chapter 8. The lesson at the heart of Chapter 9 can help you understand why you have the right to love yourself and how the Universe supports you lovingly and unconditionally. Finally, in Chapter 10, I share with you what my clients have taught me about karma, destiny, and free will.

Some Helpful Definitions

In this book I use quite a few specialized terms, some of which may be familiar to you and some that may not. Allow me to provide some helpful definitions before we begin.

The prime energy source from which all creation originates has no right or wrong name. All names we could come up with originate from within it, and so all are correct. Therefore, I will refer to it interchangeably as *God, All That Is, the One, Source, Creation, Spirit, the Infinite,* and *the Light.*

I use the word *soul* to refer to your essence, your being, your spirit, or the energy of your consciousness. Your soul projects aspects of itself into physical reality, and you know those aspects of yourself as your body and your ego, and your conscious and subconscious minds.

Every soul originates from an *Oversoul,* a composite of different souls. The Oversoul wants to experience creation in different dimensions and environments, and to do that it "splits" its energy —and each split is a different life. Each of these fragments is a whole and complete soul unto itself. Another person whose soul originates from the same Oversoul as yours is your *counterpart.*

A *soul group* is a number of Oversouls who have created close bonds with each other through their different incarnations. The members of a soul group have an agreement to help one another experience the lessons our spirits incarnate to learn.

The *levels of existence* start at the bottom with the individual soul and go all the way up to *God consciousness.* As you rise through the levels, each resonates at a higher vibration than the previous one, and the individual nature of conscious energy becomes less and less and the merging of consciousness becomes greater and greater, until you reach the One. Angelic consciousness is the first level, or split, below the energy of God, and the first to know themselves as separate and individuated beings from the one consciousness of Source. By splitting further and further into the denser vibrational realities, angelic consciousness descends into the level of the Oversoul, which further splits itself into individual souls. To imagine this structure visually, simply think of a triangle. The base represents the physical incarnations of a soul as people, and the top represents the Source. In between you find the Oversoul, and angelic consciousness above that.

During past-life regressions, I help people connect with their *Higher Self* to receive guidance and answers. Your Higher Self is an extension of your soul that exists in the higher dimensions; it is not oriented in physical reality the way your mind is. Your Higher Self holds the themes, goals, and overall vision for your current life. It carries the energy vibration of your soul, allowing you to connect and align with your vibrational essence and purpose.

Throughout this book I use the terms *past lives, simultaneous lives, other lives,* and *parallel lives* interchangeably. This is because, from the point of view of the Oversoul, all lives are taking place simultaneously in this current moment, parallel to one another. However, time is linear from our point of view, so lives taking place before the present day seem to be a "past" life. For the purposes of this book, I use all of these terms to describe what is, in truth, the same experience.

What I've just listed are basic definitions. Your understanding will deepen over the course of the book as each word is discussed in context, so don't worry if you aren't entirely clear on one or two; by the end of the book, they will be part of your vocabulary.

Exercises

Throughout *Beyond Past Lives* I offer exercises for accessing the powerful healing available to you, with or without regression. To take full advantage of the exercises, have a journal and a pen handy as you read. Take notes, but also make this book your own: Feel free to underline the sections that speak to you or highlight the sentences that move you. Write in the margins or in your journal, and express your "aha" moments. Then, share what you learn here with others. This will allow you to fully blend the energy of your consciousness with the energy of this book and create a greater plane of awareness, transformation, and growth for yourself.

I also encourage you to try past-life regression—both so you can understand the process from the inside out and because I know you will find immense value in revisiting other lives you have experienced. I have included an Appendix with a script you can use to regress yourself; please refer to it whenever you'd like. If you would rather have your regression be guided by me, I include information on where to find my audio, *Healing Through Past-Life Regression . . . and Beyond*, in the Further Resources section.

My Goal

Life is a cycle of learning and teaching. My goal in writing *Beyond Past Lives* is to share how regression has helped my clients shift to a reality of health and well-being so that you can achieve the same for yourself.

This book does not seek to delve into the validity of incarnation and regression. There are so many wonderful sources that have already explored these topics. The efficacy of this work has been established in my mind ever since my first regression. My clients and I have derived tremendous, life-changing benefits, and that is the value I want to emphasize. I will present the miraculous cases of emotional shifts, physical alignment, and transformation that my clients have gone through.

Every story told in these pages has been powerful and moving to me. As I began to write, I noticed that something bigger was going on. It felt as if this book were a project of Spirit, and I was simply a node on the big grid of Creation through which the information was pouring. Spirit was orchestrating everything. All I had to do was simply be present with each of my clients and ask the simple question, "May I share your story with others?" (*Note:* Except for Wayne and Serena Dyer, I have changed the names of my clients to protect their privacy.)

It is my hope that by sharing these stories I may show you the lessons I've learned through past-life regression, for these lessons are not merely my own; they are the lessons that all of us are learning. They speak to the challenges we all face.

I also hope that you will find support, reassurance, and new perspectives as well as new opportunities and new ways of being in the world. May this book nourish you, increase your understanding, and empower you in your growth. But most of all, may it offer you the feeling of being welcomed home—reconnection with the divinity that is already inside of you.

CHAPTER 1

EXPLORING YOUR PAST ALLOWS YOU TO HEAL YOUR PRESENT

It all began rather unassumingly. An old tooth filling had broken, so I needed to get a new one. The dentist I saw came highly recommended, yet the work he did left my mouth completely out of balance. The new filling did not fit well with the rest of my teeth and it didn't feel right when I chewed, so he did adjustment after adjustment to both the filling and the surrounding area. The numerous "fixes" left me in tremendous pain, with a condition called temporomandibular joint and muscle disorder (TMJ). There was nothing structurally wrong with my jaw, but its muscles had gotten out of alignment. I could not open my mouth without terrible discomfort, so eating became difficult. Shooting pain made my neck and shoulder muscles constantly sore. Even talking and sleeping were difficult.

I did everything I could think of to possibly remedy the situation. I started seeing a new dentist weekly for even more rounds of adjustments to ease the clenching in my muscles and allow my jaw to relax. I began sleeping with a mouth guard. I changed my pillow, and then changed my bed. I saw a physical therapist three times a week. To make chewing and eating easier, I completely changed my diet. I constantly took pills to minimize the pain and prevent infection. The list goes on and on. The whole situation was taxing my life—and my bank account—very heavily.

A year passed, and the pain still had not gone away. One day, my dentist sat me down and said, "Mira, we need to be realistic." There was no use continuing what we were doing, and it was time for me to make a choice. He suggested that I either undergo surgery or learn to live with the pain for the rest of my life. The surgery involved breaking my jaw and reattaching it with wires, and there was no guarantee that it would relieve the pain. I could not see the point in breaking something that was not broken, especially when I had been told that the problem was not in the bones and joints but in the muscles. Yet the possibility of living my life in chronic pain also scared me. Neither option seemed acceptable.

The synchronicities of life always arrange themselves. Earlier in the week, I had scheduled an appointment with the physical therapist right after my visit with the dentist. As my physical-therapy treatment began, questions arose in my mind. *Now what do I do? I've explored every possible avenue. I've done everything I could possibly do . . . or have I?* In that moment, it was as if a lightbulb went on in my mind. I remembered the regression I'd done as a child and reading about people who had miraculous physical healings after experiencing their past lives. Not knowing where else to turn, I quickly found a regressionist in New York City and scheduled an appointment.

My first session was scheduled for one hour, but we had only about 15 minutes for the actual regression, due to the time needed to get acquainted with the practitioner, share my issue, and make myself comfortable before she regressed me, and then to review what had happened before I left. (The sessions I conduct with clients today often last as long as four hours.) Because it felt very rushed and we had not yet established a level of trust, I didn't experience a past life that time. However, I was desperate for help, so I scheduled an appointment to see her again a few days later.

During my second session, I had a brief experience of a past life. I saw a picture of myself as a tall, strong black man. There was a very heavy, thick metal collar around my neck, and I had four manacles around my wrists and ankles. Chains were attached to the collar and continued down to the manacles on my wrists and feet. The metal collar was always there and incredibly uncomfortable, rubbing my jaw. I had a permanent wound in the very same spot where, in this life, I was feeling the TMJ pain. In the slave lifetime, I was quite strong physically, but inhumane treatment had broken my spirit. The dichotomy between my powerful body and the powerless spirit that occupied it was stark. I felt completely helpless. I felt no hatred toward my owners; in fact, I was grateful to them. Although they were not treating me well, they were giving me food, and I perceived that as a great kindness. I was so appreciative of it.

There in the practitioner's office, tears streamed down my face. I felt so sad for myself as this enslaved man. I felt his pain and his broken soul. How could someone treat another being in such a way? How could anyone chain another with a metal collar? How could I be so grateful to people who were clearly mistreating me— just because they were feeding me? How could I have such a strong body and yet feel completely powerless? Why didn't I speak up? Why didn't I try to change my conditions, to rebel or even escape?

The main message I brought back from the experience was the lack of personal power I had felt. As I came out of the trance and sat up on the practitioner's couch, I asked her, "What does it mean to be powerful?" She had no answer for me. (Today I use questions to guide my clients toward higher levels of understanding, but she didn't work that way.) Her response to my question was simply, "You will have to discover that on your own."

This was the only vision I had during my second session with the regressionist, and the experience was very cathartic for me. I spent the rest of the day asking myself, "What does it mean to be powerful?" No clear answers came to me, but I received emotional release along with freely flowing tears.

Looking back now, I can see that this question was central to my career experience up to that point. I was a young attorney, considered one of the most valuable members of my corporate law practice group. During every evaluation my superiors praised my work ethic, my legal skills, and my ability to manage clients and business deals. Yet they would not increase my salary to match that of my peers, and they denied my heartfelt request to switch offices even though several were available. Rather than feeling nurtured for my loyalty, I felt powerless, just like the slave had. I loved my colleagues and didn't want to lose the comfort and security I had at the firm, but I was not getting what I wanted. Speaking up hadn't helped, and persistence could potentially hurt me, so all I could do was swallow my feelings and continue being the good worker that I was.

These were the emotional issues that I was chewing on day after day, while my jaw was seeking to find relief from the pain. As I later realized (and will discuss at length in this book), all of our physical ailments begin on an emotional level. When there is discomfort in the body, it's pointing toward an idea that we need to process and resolve within ourselves. When we fail to face our challenges consciously, our bodies reflect them back to us in the form of health issues. The correlations between my struggles as the slave and my struggles in the present day are obvious now.

Although the regressionist did not ask for my jaw to be healed, the session allowed me to see that I am powerful and that I have options. The following day, I woke up without pain in my jaw for the first time in more than a year.

Very quickly my life returned to normal. I stopped taking the pain pills and sleeping with a mouth guard, and I never went back to the physical therapist. The next time I went to see the dentist, he did not know what to make of my recovery. He called my healing a miracle.

I realized I was free to make a move to another firm at any time; I did not need to repeat the pattern of powerlessness I'd experienced as the slave. I could choose instead to see myself as equal and powerful in relation to my job. This brought emotional and physical resolution to the issue, allowing me to move on.

Did I get an answer to my question about what it means to be powerful? My experience of the slave life and the situation with my employer made me realize that true power is very different from the power I had learned about in my political-science classes in school. I now know that to be powerful means to be true to who you are, rather than the domination of others. People who control and manipulate others do so only because they in fact feel *powerless*. They don't believe it is possible for them to achieve what they want without hurting themselves or others. Yet true power requires only desire, allowance, and trust. True power requires only alignment with the creative majesty of Source. To a real leader, being powerful means leading from a place of integrity and the desire to empower others.

My painful physical condition taught me this simple yet profound lesson. I learned that power comes from recognizing my true nature, and I alone can grant myself the knowing of my own powerful essence.

○

That story took place seven years ago. To this day, I continue to be pain free.

Through all those years, I never told my dentist how I healed my jaw. Back then I felt uncomfortable openly discussing my spiritual pursuits. It was enough that I was healed; I didn't feel explanations were needed. But as I was in the process of writing this book, I met with my dentist again. We hadn't seen each other in a while, so as we were catching up, I told him about my new career path. He listened with interest, and shared with me that he has a strange feeling of familiarity every time he visits the Old City of Jerusalem. He wondered out loud whether he had lived there in a different life.

His comment amazed me. Was it possible that all along my dentist had been open to spiritual discussions? Perhaps I had projected my own insecurities onto him all those years. Encouraged by his openness, I reached into my bag and pulled out a copy of my CD set, *Healing Through Past-Life Regression . . . and Beyond,* and gave it to him.

"I never told you how I healed my jaw," I said. He listened intently as I told him the story.

"I am opening a center to specialize in the healing of TMJ conditions," he told me when I'd finished. Pausing for a moment, he looked me in the eyes and said, "We should talk."

Needless to say, I left his office feeling elated for the miracle that regression has been in my life. I know it can help you, too. So let's get started by answering the most basic question you may have: What *is* past-life regression, anyway?

Past-Life Regression 101

Regression is a gentle yet powerful tool. In our sessions, I guide my clients into a state of deep physical and mental relaxation. With their bodies relaxed, their natural focus goes within, and they can access deeper states than they are able to in waking life.

We are always connected to all the lifetimes that we have lived and will live. They are part of our path, our nature, and our heritage. By letting the stimuli of the external world recede into the background, we can easily connect with the experiences that have created us. The stories, images, and feelings of those other lives are immediately present to my clients during our sessions, flowing vividly in their minds. I ask them to tell me what they perceive, and they simply narrate the story to me.

Every session is unique, yet what clients experience is always perfectly tailored to give them whatever will serve them in their highest capacity. The lifetimes are never selected at random; they're not just fun stories to tell at a dinner party. Reliving other incarnations helps us understand who we are and gives us guidance on our most pressing emotional and physical challenges. Through this simple process, people experience other lives they have lived, with many different results. Always, however, my clients leave in awe. The work I do also allows them to communicate with their Higher Selves, spirit guides, and angels; to receive guidance around important decisions; and to receive answers to lifelong questions.

Regression can help us resolve emotional and physical issues. It is helpful for understanding and releasing phobias and traumas. Through regression, we can learn about our relationships with others, and what roles those people have played in the lifetimes that we've shared. Seeing the threads between us, the connections created across time, gives us an understanding about our present-day circumstances; we can start to see with more compassion, forgiveness, and love.

The regression stories in these pages—my own and those of my clients—have revealed to me lessons about what it means to be human, how time works, the infinite possibilities of the Universe, and how to heal our most persistent emotional and physical challenges.

We don't need any special circumstances in order to experience other lifetimes. It can happen spontaneously when we find ourselves in a place or situation that reminds us of another life, and it can also happen in our dreams. That said, when we connect intentionally through regression, we can use information from our past lives to receive answers and guidance.

To the mind, the process is almost seamless. It requires only a subtle change in brain-wave activity. During a regression, we shift from a beta brain-wave state—the state characteristic of normal waking consciousness—to the alpha state, the state of relaxation. From there, and with my guidance, my clients move into either a theta or gamma state.

Theta is the state of being aware but drowsy; it's most often experienced just before falling asleep and again just before waking. Theta is the border state between conscious and unconscious. When used with intent, it is a state where profound learning, healing, and growth can take place. In the gamma state, one experiences a heightened sense of perception and consciousness, resulting in a feeling of Oneness with all—bliss and an innate understanding of the nature of existence. It is in the theta and gamma states where the powerful work of regression takes place.

To get a client into that deep level of trance, I use hypnosis. Hypnosis is such a misunderstood and feared process! Because of what we have seen during performances of stage hypnosis—and because of the claims of "mind domination" through hypnotic suggestion—our egos are naturally afraid to surrender control. What we don't understand is that reaching a deep level of trance does not need to involve the release of control over our person. During regression you will be in complete control. In fact, it's important for your ego—your mind—to be present throughout the entire session. Your mind becomes part of the process; it's the part of you that learns and understands. The new information discovered during a regression allows for your whole personality, including your ego, to shift to an expanded place of being and creating life.

All hypnosis is really self-hypnosis. In the process of relaxation, the ego mind determines that my client's body—the person—is safe in its physical surroundings; that it is safe to relax into the serenity and comfort of my office and my presence because I am someone who can be trusted to guide them and take good care of them. The moment the ego determines that it will be safe during its explorations, the mind is able to orient itself.

Hypnosis is the ability to focus within. By relaxing the body, our focus can shift from the input of the external senses to the input of the *inner* senses. The mind disentangles from physical reality and gives the inner senses freedom to go beyond and explore. Next, the inner senses naturally orient themselves and travel up through the different layers of consciousness—through emotions, through personal beliefs, through the shared social beliefs and constructs, and through the Higher Self. The higher our psychic energy rises, the freer we are from our personality and the story of our life. The higher our vibration rises, the closer we come to merging with the consciousness of our Oversoul.

As I discussed, our Oversoul is the "mother" of all the souls that have inhabited our present, past, and future lives. It exists in a dimension where all time is experienced as *now*. To the Oversoul, what you and I call "past," "present," and "future" is all happening in the same moment. During a regression, we allow our inner senses to reach the dimension of the Oversoul; we merge our consciousness with its consciousness. From that dimension, we are able to plunge back down and experience the physical reality of any life we choose. This is why, when we relive a lifetime, we fully identify *as* that person. We are perceiving that life from the position of our Oversoul, which is one with all the souls it creates. During a regression, we know ourselves as that "other" life as well as "this" life because both lives are simultaneously taking place on two separate tracks of our Oversoul's energy and activity. All of our lives appear as "now" to the Oversoul; consequently, that is how we experience them during regression.

Therefore, regression is not really the experience of a memory. Sure, we can call it that for the sake of convenience; that's what we're doing when we refer to our other lives as "past" lives. But if we truly want to understand what occurs during regression, we need to acknowledge that we are connecting our vibrational energy with that of our Oversoul—and from there we merge with other lives that are unfolding in the present, now moment. This is a very novel understanding of the regression process and the nature of existence. The lessons on time in Chapter 6 will allow you to better understand this truth, and to appreciate the power of these explorations we call "past-life regressions."

Life Lessons

Regression is one of the most effective paths for learning our life lessons. When we connect with other lifetimes we have lived, we are able to experience for ourselves the struggles, joys, emotions, and details of our story. Souls like to incarnate with other souls with whom they have created bonds in prior lives so that they can continue growing and exploring together. Because of this, during regression we often meet loved ones and friends as well as people with whom we have challenging relationships.

The life we experience during a regression will always share a common theme with the life we're living now. By reliving another life, we get the benefit of a different perspective on how to handle a lesson we may be struggling with. That is the power of this process: We see the bigger picture, the tapestry that has been weaved through different lifetimes. In doing so, we get a deep and profound understanding of our soul's path. When we see how we handled the same challenges in our other lives, we have the ability to do things differently now. We free ourselves. We empower ourselves. This is how exploring past lives allows us to heal our present, both physically and emotionally.

Now let's take a look at the life lessons my clients have taught me—and the possibilities these lessons offer to transform *your* life.

CHAPTER 2

ALL LIVES ARE SIMULTANEOUS

One day a few years ago, while I was still working as a corporate lawyer, I decided to stop by a Barnes & Noble near my office. It was lunchtime, and I wanted to see whether there were any books that might catch my eye before heading back to work. As I browsed through the shelves in the New Age section, I saw one of my favorites, *The Nature of Personal Reality* by Jane Roberts. The book felt good in my hands when I took it off the shelf; then, just as I began to open it, a thought popped into my mind.

Put your personal card in the book.

I had learned not to question such moments of intuition, but to follow them with playful curiosity. However, even *I* had to admit that this thought made no sense. Still, I reached in my purse, pulled out a card, and tucked it between the pages. As I put the book back on the shelf, another thought came up.

Whoever buys this book and finds your card will be a very special person.

This thought felt foreign, as if it came from someone else—someone who knew much more than I did. There was a sense of something mystical surrounding the words *very special person.* My soul recognized the feeling, but my mind could not explain it.

Months later, after I had completely forgotten about the incident, I received an e-mail from a man named John. He explained that he had gotten the feeling that it was time to read *The Nature of Personal Reality* again. So he went to the same Barnes & Noble I had gone to, across the street from his own workplace. He picked up the very same copy of the book I'd had in my hands, and my card fell out.

Who cares? he said to himself. But for reasons unbeknownst to him, he kept the card anyway. When he got home that night, he visited my website. After reading for just a few minutes, he e-mailed me. Something was pushing him to do it, he said; it was almost automatic.

Among the thousands and thousands of words on my website, one phrase had made an impression on John. In a blog entry I had written six months earlier, I'd mentioned that at work I felt like "a spirit undercover." At that time, I was still working as a corporate lawyer in a large firm on Park Avenue. I was good at my job, but as a "good lawyer" I felt that I couldn't share my private spiritual interests—and therefore, my true personality—with my colleagues. I was afraid that I would be judged, misunderstood, ostracized, or worse. It was that feeling of being alone that made me feel like a spirit undercover—I was working covertly to bring positive energy, cooperation, balance, and light to the office, where such qualities were not given priority. John recognized the same feelings in himself, so he reached out to me. He wanted to find a soul to share with—someone who understood. I definitely did!

John told me that he was a single man in his mid-20s who had embarked on a spiritual path a few years before but felt very lonely with no family or friends walking beside him. I then shared my experiences with past-life regression, explaining that what people learn during regression is always perfectly aligned with where they are and provides healing in the most unexpected ways. In my excitement, I offered to regress him, and he was curious enough to say yes.

I had been passionately talking about regression with every family member and friend I could, and I had regressed many of them. But with John it was different; I'd just met him, after all. When our appointment came, I was nervous. My voice was shaky as I began guiding him into calming his body. Luckily, as I relaxed him, I too began to relax. I had no idea that I was about to encounter the first—and perhaps the most surprising—lesson I would learn from past-life regression.

He Said What?!

After I helped John go within himself, I asked him to tell me what he saw, felt, and heard. He described standing in front of a barbershop on a cobblestone street. He commented that the lampposts on the street had shades. He was wearing a suit—brown pants, a vest, a striped shirt, and a brown jacket. To complete the ensemble, he had on dress shoes and a hat he described as a "newspaper boy's cap." He was in his early 30s, and his name in that life was John, too. (Although he had different names in the lifetimes we went through, I will continue to refer to him simply as John to make it easier to follow.)

The session continued with me asking John various questions. When telling me about the development of his life, John was very specific with names and dates. He was a successful banker living in Brooklyn, New York, and he had a son and a daughter with his wife, Katherine. We saw the birth of his son in 1940 and scenes from his daughter's wedding in 1963. We discovered that his son was killed in a car accident in 1957. John remembered thinking on his daughter's wedding day that she could have found a better husband. Over the years, he and his daughter lost touch, and life became very lonely when his wife died in 1971. After years of feeling cut off from the world, and then losing his fortune due to poor investment decisions, John committed suicide in 1978.

The main lesson John was meant to learn in that lifetime was about loneliness and the consequences of suicide (which we will discuss at much greater length in Chapter 6). After John's soul rose from his body, he went to the spirit side and was met by his spirit guide. John and his guide discussed the need for him to be reborn and to confront the issues of loneliness he was unable to bear during the life he'd just abruptly ended. He experienced himself being reborn very quickly . . . and told me that the year was 1950.

He said what?! the question screamed in my mind. *Oh, my God!*

A wave of panic and disbelief washed over me. John was lying on the bed in front of me, and I was sitting on a nearby chair, trying to hide my shock. We'd just relived the life in which he was born in the early 20th century and died in 1978—and now he was telling me that in his next life he was born in 1950!

My mind protested. *No, no, no! This is impossible! This is not how time works. This is not how reincarnation works! Time is linear. Only after a soul completes one life does it go on to another. None of this makes sense!*

I was in a state of shock. I attempted to stop breathing and disappear into the chair. I was afraid my very breath would betray me, and he would sense my panic. I worried that my racing thoughts would influence him and interrupt the scenes flowing through his mind.

The silence seemed to last an eternity. My heart was hammering in my chest.

John's words continued to reverberate through my mind, and I thought, *What do I do? What should I say?*

Just wait, said a voice from deep within me. *Let him speak first.*

I waited. The lack of air was hurting my lungs. I attempted to take the quietest breath I had ever inhaled. Thankfully, John broke the silence.

"She is showing me off to her girlfriends," he said. "So many women . . . too much perfume, too much makeup. I am crying. I don't like this at all. . . ."

I took a deep breath, relieved that he had continued narrating what he saw. John told me that in this second life he was a mixed-race child in the South who had been adopted by a rich white family. John's parents had been trying to have a child for a while before they settled on adoption, yet his father could not accept that his son had darker skin. They never became close, and John was always afraid of him.

One day, when John was four years old, he came home with a black eye. He had been beaten up at school by kids who made fun of him for being adopted. His parents began fighting about it, his father insisting that they never should have adopted him. This became a point of contention, and when John was 13 years old, his parents divorced.

John and his mother moved to New York City. He befriended other boys who were darker skinned like him; they formed a doo-wop group and sang on the corner in front of the local candy store. John was not interested in studying, so he became a construction worker and was integrated into an all-white construction crew. He really liked a girl named Suzanne, who wanted to marry him and have a family. But John felt that since he was just in his 20s, he was too young to marry. He traveled to Los Angeles and never went back to New York.

There were many incredible events in John's second life, yet none of them seemed to affect him emotionally. In fact, he did not seem interested in very many things. I noticed that he wasn't too concerned about civil rights, being adopted, his parents' fighting, or going to school.

In California, John led a very simple life. He worked, ate, and slept, and was generally content. But the thought of not marrying Suzanne pained him every single day. Looking at the last days of his life, John said to me, "I am really old. I am in my 90s. I live in a nursing home in California. I spend most of my time sitting there, staring at the window. Time wasted . . ."

From our present-day point of view, John was experiencing both a past life *and a future life*. Given that in this life he was born in 1950 and was seeing himself in his 90s, it was clear that the nursing-home scene was some time in the 2040s. To make matters even more perplexing, John—as the person he is today—was born in the mid-1980s. This adventure in timelessness continued through four more lives, all of which took place in roughly the same 130-year period—between the 1910s and 2040s.

John's Other Life Plans

After John's second life he realized that, by living his life *so* simply, he hadn't learned anything. The time spent in that incarnation felt like wasted time, and he decided next to experience a life that would teach him how to love.

In this third life he was born in Tennessee on July 3, 1946. (I noted the date in my mind, still wondering how he was having all these overlapping lives.) John had a large family, but he was closest with his twin sister, Jan. She was a tomboy, while he was timid, emotional, and very studious. Growing up, Jan was one of the pretty girls in school. John described himself as a dork, but nobody picked on him because of his sister. Half of the guys liked her and the other half were afraid of her.

The first time John and Jan lived apart was when they went to college. He went to the Massachusetts Institute of Technology (MIT), and she went to the University of California, Los Angeles (UCLA). In his second year of school, John learned that his sister had been raped by a man from her college. There was no question in John's mind what he needed to do, so he dropped out of MIT and moved to Los Angeles to take care of her. He was happy that he could be there for her.

One day, shortly after arriving in California in 1967, he was rushing home to bring Jan something from the bakery and was fatally hit by a car as he crossed the street. His sister could not bear losing him so soon after undergoing the trauma of rape, so she swallowed a handful of pills and committed suicide.

After John's soul went to the spirit side, he did not reincarnate immediately, but waited for Jan. She created a new life plan that allowed her to integrate the emotional issues that had caused her suicide. After she successfully completed that life, they were ready to be born again together. What followed is a story that always melts my heart.

In this fourth life, John was a young musician in New York City. He was single, and his parents had passed on and he had no siblings. Every night after practice with his jazz band, he would stop by a diner near his home to grab a bite and hopefully sneak a peek at this waitress he liked. He was shy and nervous by nature, so even though the waitress would always smile at him, he never really talked to her.

One day John finally gathered the courage to introduce himself, and she said her name was Lauren. He asked if she would like to get a cup of coffee with him, and she said yes. She told him to come back at midnight when her shift ended, but he fell asleep while waiting for the appointed hour to come. When he woke up at 3 A.M. he panicked, worried that he had missed her. He rushed to the diner to find that she was still waiting for him. She pretended to scold him but in truth she was very happy to see him. Their relationship developed quickly, and within six months they were married.

Lauren went back to school and became a teacher. She and John never had children, but they did everything together and really enjoyed one another. They went to Paris for their honeymoon and had a great time. For their 25th anniversary they went back to the "City of Light," and although they were a lot older, it was no different. Lauren was always goofy, and because she never cared what others thought, John was able to let go and have fun. Then she passed away from breast cancer, and John was left alone. I asked him whether it was difficult for him. He said, "It wasn't as bad as you'd think. We had so many memories. We did so many things." A year later he died from a heart attack.

As he was drifting away from the scenes of that life, John said to me, "Her name was Lauren, right? I always knew there was something else, but I could never put my finger on it. She was really Jan." Our names and relationships may change, but the love we have for one another always brings us together, life after life.

When he went to the spirit side, John met his guide, who was always there awaiting his return. This time, his spirit guide showed him that it was time for him to teach. John hesitated but took the opportunity to do just that in his fifth life.

He was born on an Army base in Texas during the Vietnam War. His mother was always worried that her son would grow up without a father, and sure enough, John's father did end up being killed in the war. Here again, John gave another time marker with the Vietnam War, which meant that his fifth life also overlapped in time with his other lives.

Following the passing of his father, John and his mother moved to New York City. John remarked that even though he was close to his mom, she was more focused on her fears than on the quality of their relationship. He was a good son, an all-American kid: good in school, good at sports, good-looking, and popular. As he grew up he became very successful in the financial world, but his love was art. He loved drawing and writing poems and stories.

John's mother never really liked any of the girls he dated. He said, "God forbid if I were to go out with somebody. I would feel bad. She always seems so worried anyway, so I don't want to worry her more." John spent the last couple of years of his life with a sweet woman named Nancy, and his mother had to accept that Nancy would have to do. John passed away in his sleep when he was in his early 40s, and his mother started a school fund with his money. Because she did not have to worry about him anymore after his death, John remarked that she was doing better.

Once John transitioned into spirit after this life he recognized that he didn't really teach anyone anything. Determined to do better, for his sixth life his soul chose a life in Japan, in which he was a girl named Kiyomi. Kiyomi's parents passed on during a car accident and she was left to take care of her younger sister. Kiyomi became pretty successful—a well-known music producer who also owned a chain of restaurants—and she continuously donated her money because she believed it was not good to have too much. John relived the sixth life very quickly. The scenes were fast-forwarding through his mind, and because of that he did not give me any dates during this regression. Later, I asked him to ascertain the time period for what he'd seen and he said that the life had taken place around 1980 to 2010.

Once in spirit, John was greeted by his guide, who said to him, "It's good that you gave your money away, but what did you teach? Giving the money away didn't teach anyone anything."

John recognized that something was missing because he had not done a good job of teaching.

John had relived six lifetimes, and I knew it was time that we invite his Higher Self to speak to us. I was eager to ask how it was possible that all six lifetimes had taken place in the same 130-year period!

Parallel Lives

Once clients see their other lifetimes, I use my guidance to help them expand their consciousness and connect to the highest levels of love, light, and healing. I then converse with the Higher Self about all the issues and challenges the person is facing in his or her present life.

The Higher Self is the nonphysical extension of us—the part that knows the bigger picture and is always there to guide us to our greatest and most fulfilling life. By merging the mind's energy with the vibrations of the Higher Self, we *become* our Higher Self.

When I connected John with the energy of his Higher Self, I wanted to know how it was that all six lifetimes he experienced were taking place simultaneously. Here is an edited transcript of what I heard:

Mira: In the lifetimes we explored today, the lives were over-lapping in time. It really doesn't match up with how we people think about time. How is John supposed to think of them?

John: It is really just a matter of accepting. He is half-in and half-out. Half-holding-on-to-what-is-normal and half-not. That is what's causing the divide between the thinking that time is linear and time as nothing.

Mira: What is time, then?

John: Time is infinite.

Mira: So does it serve any purpose that we people think in terms of time?

John: It works for Earth. It's needed for you guys.

Mira: Can you explain parallel lives to me, because I would like to deepen my understanding. Does a soul split into these different lives simultaneously? Does the main soul stay where it is?

John: Yes. A fragment soul goes to every one of those experiences.

Mira: Were all these real experiences?

John: They were all real because the main soul still experiences all of them.

Although I had never heard this before, it felt familiar—like something I had long forgotten. It felt as if I had remembered a great truth that had been lost through the centuries. John's Higher Self explained that time is a concept that works for people on Earth, but beyond our realm time is infinite. To us it may seem that lifetimes are consecutive, but in truth all the lives an Oversoul experiences are occurring simultaneously.

We are multidimensional. There is so much more to us than what our five senses tell us. It is through the adventure of living and opening up to all other realms of our being that we become more and more aware of the magnificent creation that we are.

John's Higher Self explained that every incarnation is a fragment of the Oversoul. As I mentioned in Chapter 1, the Oversoul is an energy consciousness that is comprised of all the souls you have ever been and ever will be. It creates fragments of itself because it desires to know itself by experiencing life from many different perspectives. When the Oversoul chooses to learn about a specific theme—let's say the lesson of love—it creates energy splits of itself, or different lives, each of which explore and experience love.

No learning of a lesson is complete if it is one-sided. One could never know about love without learning about abandonment and loneliness, for example. The Oversoul learns just as much about the theme of love by experiencing a life full of loving, nurturing relationships as it does by experiencing one full of relationship dysfunction. Only by studying every perspective does the Oversoul gain the full knowledge and experience of a subject.

This is the nature of the Oversoul. This also is the nature of All That Is: to create, and to expand its awareness through its creations. Every fragment formed by the Oversoul is a soul in itself.

Even though we speak of individual souls as fragments of the Oversoul, it is important to note that each soul is complete and whole unto itself. This point was made evident to me during a later regression I had with a client named Lisa (you will read more about her later in the book). Lisa also experienced lives that overlapped in time, and her Higher Self explained that even though each soul is a fragment, there is nothing lacking about any of them. Each soul itself has consciousness and the ability to exercise its free will, choosing its experiences in the different dimensions of existence. Despite fragmenting itself, the Oversoul is whole and complete. Just as every drop in the ocean has the properties of the entire ocean, so does the soul as it relates to the Oversoul.

This understanding also provides an explanation of the structure of existence. The fragments that compose an Oversoul are called "counterpart souls" because they are one another's counterparts, sharing the same Oversoul signature vibration. A group of Oversouls comprises a soul group. During each of the next levels of existence, the Oversoul resonates at a higher vibration than it did during the previous level of existence, and the individual nature of the counterpart souls diminishes. Simultaneously, the merging of consciousness becomes greater and greater all the way to the One.

Therefore, at the highest vibrational level, you and I—and all human beings who live and have lived on the planet—are part of the same Oversoul, the same one energy we call God. From that perspective, we people share an Oversoul with rocks, plants, animals, and water. We all stem from the same profound love. We are all brothers and sisters.

All Incarnations Exist Simultaneously

An Oversoul creates its fragment souls in order to grow through them, and all of these different souls exist simultaneously. To put this in a simple analogy, you can think of the souls as the fingers of a hand that all exist and function at the same moment in time, while the hand itself is the Oversoul. Another image is that of a train and its cars. The train's cars all travel on the track simultaneously, each holding its unique passengers, activities, and conversations, just like the separate lives. Together they form the train, or the consciousness that comprises the Oversoul.

To explore specific themes and grow to its fullest potential, an Oversoul may choose a very large span of time as its playground; its soul lives could take place over hundreds of years. When revisited during a regression, these lives tend to be consecutively ordered, with no overlap in time, so we feel that we're purely experiencing "past" lives. The progression of the lives thus seems to fit into our linear understanding of time. As was the case with John, however, it may serve the Oversoul better to explore its themes and create all its lives in a short span of Earth time. When those lives are revisited during a regression session, we experience some or all of these lives as overlapping in time, just as John experienced his parallel lives. This is the profound learning that John's session gave me: the lives that the souls create all exist in the same concurrent moment. From the point of view of the Oversoul, all incarnations are happening simultaneously, in this very moment! Lives are not past, present, or future—they are simultaneous.

People previously thought that the cycle of reincarnation operated as follows: A soul is born, and incarnates. Its body dies eventually, and the soul returns to the dimension between lives. There it determines how well it did in life, and then chooses to be born again in order to work on the same or different lessons. The cycle continues from there until the soul perfects itself and merges with God consciousness. In other words, we saw reincarnation as the linear progression of a singular soul. We used to think of any "other" lives as "past lives" of the same one person. Future lives were hardly ever looked into because, according to our understanding, the future hadn't happened yet.

But because our minds are now able to better process multidimensional thinking in space and time, we are ready to transcend these simpler explanations offered by so many generations of our predecessors. Outside the dimension of our Earth reality, time operates by a different pattern. It is not linear—it is simply and always now. Thus, each life is both *still unfolding* and *has already been completed* in the present moment.

John's session was a true spiritual education for me. The concept of parallel lives is novel within the world of past-life regression; in fact, it's on the cutting edge of our spiritual awareness as a whole. During my session with John I felt like an explorer, venturing into uncharted dimensions of knowledge. At the time I was not aware of any other regressionist who had come across this information in his or her work. Up until that point, I hadn't read any books that talked about the simultaneity of existence. If I had encountered it somewhere, it had flown over my head without my understanding the concept or consciously processing it. Not to mention that John was my very first client outside of my beloved family and friends! I felt immense gratitude that Spirit had deemed me ready to facilitate a session of such great importance.

After my session with him, I wanted to tell the whole world about parallel lives, but I was hesitant. Who was I to revolutionize our understanding of reincarnation? After all, I was a corporate lawyer representing publicly traded companies—not a spiritual guru!

Yet, every chance I had, I shared my findings. You could hear the enthusiasm in my voice whenever I talked about the simultaneity of existence. My revelations prompted inspired conversations wherever I went. Talking about John's regressions—and the truth about how our lives operate—filled me with great excitement. In those moments, I felt I was locking into the energy of my true self, that I was fulfilling my purpose of inspiring people and bringing light into their lives.

In time, I realized that both the world and I were ready to share this information. I now know that I am always given what

I am ready for, and only when I am ready for it. By allowing myself to share my discoveries, I have grown into the person I am today—a person who can stand up and present new ideas to the world. Spirit never doubted me, and was only lovingly waiting for me to gain the confidence to share what I have learned.

It is clear to me that the Universe is yearning for this new shift in thinking. Everywhere, people are taking steps in the direction of the Light. We are making great progress in assimilating and applying subtle metaphysical knowledge. And, most important, we are stepping out of our comfort zones to rediscover life in new and exciting ways. The understanding that time is simultaneous can assist all of us in our spiritual progression and expand our awareness of how we create our own realities.

Conscious Awareness of Concurrent Lives

You may wonder why you aren't consciously aware of other concurrent lives you are living. The explanation lies in our brain's capacity to process information. Neurologically, we are only able to tune in to the present life we know; it helps us maintain a coherent sense of self. How confused our egos would be if they were able to simultaneously receive input from all of our counterparts! Our brains filter out a large amount of information surrounding us in our daily lives as it is: of the 400 *billion* bits of information our brains process every second, we are aware of only 2,000.

Imagine what it would be like to have an input even a few times that! The information would overwhelm us, leaving us incapacitated. One might wonder, *Am I a factory worker in Harbin, China? A camel-riding Bedouin? An ancient Hawaiian kahuna? Who am I?* Rare are the cases where people are consciously aware of the other fields of existence where they dwell. Children are sometimes able to spontaneously connect to other lives, but even in those circumstances the input is brief. They may receive a burst of information in one moment, and in the next moment reorient to the reality they know as their own. People may also connect with other lifetimes in dreams, because the dream state provides a safe container for the ego to explore.

Even though we're not consciously aware of it, we are constantly communicating with our counterparts and our Oversoul. We are subconsciously always in touch, and we communicate in our dreams. And even though we don't consciously recognize it, we are forever being influenced by the lives of our counterparts. Their preferences, experiences, thoughts, and conclusions affect us. We learn from the ways they explore their themes, and they learn from us. We assist each other. It might show up as unexplainable attractions toward particular types of music, foreign countries, or foods. For me, it is the love of miso soup. I could eat miso soup for breakfast, lunch, and dinner, day after day, and never tire of it. It came as no surprise to discover that my Oversoul has created a life in Japan that I strongly connect with, which is exploring similar themes to my life here and now.

Exercise: The Influence of Your Counterparts

Once you understand the simultaneous lives of counterpart souls, it is very easy to recognize their influences. Certain feelings, ideas, moments of inspiration, and different points of view start to stand out as connections with your other lives.

In this exercise, you will be exploring such influences through journaling, so be sure to have a journal and pen close at hand. Start by finding a quiet place where you can sit comfortably for at least 20 minutes. Take a few deep breaths, and connect with your body. Notice what you're feeling right now. If there are lots of thoughts and emotions swirling around, just watch them and release them. Then, once you feel ready, pick up your journal and answer the following questions in writing:

- What are some unexplainable likes and dislikes you have? Things your parents found interesting about you, which none of your siblings or friends shared?

- Do you have skills or abilities that are unexplainable based on the story of your life?

- Do you have an affinity for a particular language or culture? A particular food? A particular type of music?

- Do you feel pulled toward a particular place? Once you're there, does it feel familiar, like you know how to navigate around it?

- Are you fascinated with a particular time in history?

- Are there causes you are fervently passionate about?

- What kind of books did you love reading as a child?

- When you were young did you talk to your parents about your other families and other lifetimes?

- Do you have intense phobias and fears with no reasonable explanation?

- Do you have any recurring dreams?

Once you've answered these questions, let your imagination run free. What could each of these influences be pointing toward? What lives might your Oversoul counterparts be living right now? In which time periods? In which countries? Don't censor yourself; this is simply an open exploration of possibility. Have fun imagining how different your lives might be.

Finally, write for a few minutes about what thoughts and emotions come up for you when you consider that these influences might be coming from your Oversoul counterparts. Do you feel excited? Relieved? Frightened? Unsure? Whatever you're feeling, write it down.

There Is Only One Life

During a regression, as the images, feelings, and impressions begin to flow, we intuitively identify who we are in the parallel life we're experiencing. We become that "other" version of ourselves. We see, hear, smell, sense, know, and feel from the perspective of that person; we speak from the first person "I." We are able to instantly recognize our counterparts and identify with them because souls that originate from the same Oversoul vibrate with the same unique identifying frequency.

When we regress to another life, we tune in to the energy and experiences of that being. We essentially *become* that other person. We connect to another extension of our own soul, which has similar vibrations and is exploring similar themes. The experience feels deeply personal, as if we are also feeling all that joy and all that pain. This makes sense, because the life is experienced through and belongs to the Oversoul, and thus belongs to us. In reality we are all one, so when we project our consciousness into a situation and tune in to a particular person, we literally *become* that person.

It is common for someone who is describing a regression experience to say, "In my past life, I was . . ." This is a convenient shortcut, and from a certain point of view it is correct. We are all composed of the energy of our Oversoul. As a result, any life created by the Oversoul is part of us, too.

Yet it is also important to understand that your present life is your only life. This life is the only life the Oversoul has created through your unique soul. In truth, you do not have past lives. You do not have future lives. You are a unique expression of consciousness that is only appearing now. No other being will ever be you, nor will you ever be any other being. These two perspectives may seem paradoxical at first, but if you let it sink in for a bit, you will see that they can exist side by side.

You may wonder why a person experiences a particular life during a regression. For clients and me, the process seems automatic. I advise clients to trust the intelligence of their expanded self and the organizing force of the Universe. Their soul is already communicating with their soul counterparts; it knows what will be most beneficial and important for a client to see at that moment. As a result, the lives the person tunes in to are always relevant. The client's takeaway is always appropriate, always healing, and always guiding.

The other simultaneous lives of your Oversoul are not static and frozen in time. Even though we think of those lives that took place prior to this moment as having passed in linear time, those lives are not "over." They very much exist and are presently developing. Therefore, it is very natural and normal that your counterparts would be sharing ideas and experiences outside of your conscious awareness. However, your conscious mind is capable of recognizing the thoughts and feelings that come as a result of the sharing. This is very much like talking to a friend or a sibling on the phone. When you talk, you tell each other stories and give each other support and advice. And when you hang up you recognize that the other person's energy has had an effect on you. You feel a bit different, and you think a bit differently for having talked to him or her.

These moments of recognition are a wonderful way to remind yourself that you are always supported and always guided on your journey. It is powerful to remind yourself that you exist and function on many levels of reality, that you truly are multidimensional.

All consciousness exists at once. All lives created by an Oversoul exist in the same one eternal moment. You can think of time as a filter through which consciousness expresses itself on our planet. As such, some lives are created in what we perceive as different historic moments, or periods. An Oversoul can create lives at the time of Christ, during the Crusades, or during the Industrial Revolution, depending on its objectives. Therefore, people having a regression may experience these other lives as taking place at a different historic moment than their own incarnation. This choice is made by the Oversoul, depending on the themes it is looking to explore and what best serves its growth.

Are There Counterparts on Earth?

If an Oversoul can choose to create several separate lives in the same historic timeframe, you may wonder whether you have soul counterparts living on Earth right now. The answer to that question is: maybe! Such counterparts are two or more people who have the same soul vibration and originate from the same Oversoul. You may even know your counterparts—they could be your lovers, your friends, or your enemies.

A client of mine saw a life where she was the male stable manager on a large estate. The man was very proud of his position and how smoothly everything ran. One day the lady of the house and her husband wanted to go for a ride, so the manager prepared the horses. Unbeknownst to him, the horse he chose for the lady of the house had an inflammation in its leg and was not feeling well. The manager sensed that something was not quite right, but he chose to send the horse out anyway to maintain his reputation. While riding, the horse tripped, fell, and killed the lady of the manor. The stable manager was executed for this accident. As the story of the life was unfolding, my client became aware that she was both the stable manager *and* the lady who got killed. Their Oversoul created two lives that interacted so it could simultaneously learn the lessons of tuning in, paying attention, and being responsible for yourself and others from two points of view.

Another regressionist shared with me a session with a man who experienced a life where he was a corrupt, violent, and generally unpleasant person. In that life, the man was married to a wife who, despite all his shortcomings, always loved him and cared for him. It was revealed during the regression that both the husband and the wife were fragments of the same Oversoul. The Oversoul had chosen to create those two lives on opposite sides of the marriage in order to experience the family dynamic from both perspectives simultaneously. And Seth, an entity channeled by author Jane Roberts, identified Jane and her husband, Robert Butts, as counterparts. In *The "Unknown" Reality*, Seth reveals that Jane and Robert are "each playing out 'opposite' aspects of each other, yet merging for common purposes and goals."

In *Conversations with Seth*, Susan Watkins details the adventures of consciousness that she and other ESP class members had under the guidance of Jane Roberts. In the class, the idea of concurrent-life counterparts was examined, and Seth shared with some of the participants whom their counterparts are. Susan learned that Jane Roberts, Zelda Graydon, and Richard Bach, the author of *Jonathan Livingston Seagull,* were her counterparts. To better understand their interconnectedness and how their experiences fed into the growth of their Oversoul, Susan went on to examine the similarities and differences the four of them shared.

Our counterparts may be of a similar or different age, gender, ethnic background, religious system, or socioeconomic status. Similarities and differences between counterparts reflect a soul's chosen approach to its Oversoul's theme. Our counterparts may share a path very similar to ours and we may call them friends and lovers. We may meet other counterparts coincidentally, we may pass them on the street without even noticing, or we may never have contact with them at all. We might dislike or feel judgmental toward our counterparts' personalities and choices. We may have counterparts with ethnic, cultural, or political backgrounds that we vehemently oppose. None of this makes us any less connected. In truth, we are all interrelated; there are no strangers on Earth.

Exercise: How to Identify Your Counterparts

By now, I'm sure you're wondering which of the people in your life may actually be your counterparts. When doing this exercise I caution you not to let any romantic notion—having a counterpart who completes you in an intimate relationship, for example—affect your intuitive knowing. As breathtaking as the fairy tale of having your partner be your counterpart may be, such ideas may prevent you from seeing the true soul connections with your lovers and the people around you.

In *The "Unknown" Reality,* Seth gives advice on how to identify your counterparts:

I have spoken about counterparts in [Jane Roberts's] class. Many of the students became deadly serious as they tried to understand the concept. Some wanted me to identify their counterparts for them. One student . . . said little. He let his own creative imagination go wherever it might while he held the general idea in mind. He played with the concept, then. In a way his experiences were like those of a child—open, curious, filled with enthusiasm. As a result he himself discovered a few of his counterparts. Most people, however, are so utterly serious that they suspect their own creativity.

When you're ready to connect with your counterparts, do so in the spirit of playfulness and curiosity. Set aside 20 minutes when you know you will not be disturbed. Sit in a comfortable positing, with a journal nearby. Take a deep breath in, hold it, and then slowly let it out. Do this two more times and become aware of how more and more relaxed your body becomes. Next, set the intention that you will connect with your soul counterparts. Release any expectation about what it will be like, and even needing to know the answer. Instead, notice what images and thoughts come up. Are you drawn to particular places or to particular people?

As Seth suggests, approach this exercise with the lightheartedness of a child. Remember, needing to be right is not important. Use your imagination freely. If you were to imagine who your counterparts are, who would you imagine them being? Trust yourself; deep within you, you already know. You already have all this information. Continue to let the question *Who are my counterparts?* float freely in your mind, noticing what thoughts and images come up. Then, when you feel ready, slowly bring your consciousness to the present moment.

Write down any thoughts, feelings, images, and ideas that came to you. If anyone you know came to you as a possible counterpart, spend a little time journaling about the similarities or dissimilarities between you. What were your childhoods like? Are you of the same gender or socioeconomic status? Did you have similar religious upbringings? Do you have common interests or challenges? Are you working through similar lessons each in your own way?

If the images that came to you were of a stranger, acknowledge how connected in Oneness we all really are.

Complete this process by sending through your heart an energetic ball of love to those people, thanking them for being part of your soul's expansion.

Having this experience will provide another glimpse of the marvelous, multifaceted being that you are.

I have already shared some mind-expanding ideas with you. The understanding that the life experiences of our souls are "simultaneous lives" and not "past lives" is novel. Allow me now to take you even further in our explorations of consciousness and present the idea of parallel realities of your *possible selves*. In the next chapter, I will introduce you to this idea through one of my most intense and moving personal regression experiences. As with all adventures, this is a story of challenges, dangers, passionate love, and great learning.

CHAPTER 3

EVERY CHOICE CREATES A NEW REALITY

I grew up in Communist Bulgaria. Because atheism is a core value of the Communist ideology, every effort was made to marginalize and eradicate the presence of the Bulgarian Orthodox Church in everyday life. As a result, religion and mysticism were simply not a part of my early childhood years. I was never told about God, angels, or the eternity of my soul.

In the late 1980s, the democratic revolution swept through Eastern Europe like a wave. I vividly remember the night of November 10, 1989. I was sitting on the sofa watching TV with my parents, a few hours after the Berlin Wall had fallen. During a live broadcast of the meeting of the Central Committee of the Bulgarian Communist Party, our country's President—who had held the office for 35 years—was forced to resign. The camera showed the utter shock on the President's face so clearly. My dad, who was sitting to my right, jumped up and yelled in disbelief. My mom, who was sitting on my left, also voiced her surprise. They looked at each other and then at the TV. I was just nine years old and couldn't really understand what was going on. Even so, I knew it was important—very, very important.

Many social and economic changes resulted from that internal coup. One of them was the influx of religious and metaphysical ideas. Because they had been denied for so long, people were thirsty for this kind of knowledge. Spiritual information of every kind became readily available. Going to church on Easter became acceptable, as did talking about energy healing and poltergeists.

I was 13 years old when I first stumbled on to my purpose and passion: past-life regression. My uncle Veselin Pasliev was reading *Through Time Into Healing* by Brian Weiss, and my interest was immediately piqued. I couldn't wait for him to finish so that I could claim it for myself. My eagerness seemed inexplicable back then, but now I see that the book was an early signpost marking my path in this life. Even though the concept of reincarnation was new to me, I did not question the possibility. It just seemed so natural, so normal. As Voltaire said, "It is not more surprising to be born twice than once; everything in nature is resurrection."

I loved the stories and wisdom in Brian's book. I loved the possibilities it offered. I loved it so much that upon reading the final few pages, I decided to record myself reading his sample script and experience a regression for myself. I remember thinking, *I am only 13. There is really nothing wrong with me. I have no phobias. I have no physical ailments. Why would I do this?* But the pull was too strong to resist.

I made the recording, rewound the tape to the beginning, and even though I did not know what to expect, pressed PLAY. The recording guided me through a beautiful relaxation, and I felt very calm and comfortable. At the moment I crossed through time into another life, however, all that changed.

I immediately dropped into the body of a woman who was running for her life. I became her, and my heart was pounding with fear. My breath became short, abrupt, and desperate. I was terrified. I was running down a dimly lit hallway because there were men chasing me who would kill me if they caught me. I was dressed in a jacket and skirt made of thick, gray wool, along with black stockings and black shoes with small heels. My dark hair was neatly tucked in a bun in the back.

The sound of my steps reverberated against the brick walls as I ran. There were rows of doors on both sides, and I was hastily trying to open them, one after another. All were locked. At the very end of the hallway I finally found a door handle that gave in. As I entered the room, I saw that it was bare. There was only one small window with bars on it, and it was high on the wall, close to the ceiling. There was no way out. I knew I was trapped. I knew they would catch me.

I also knew the circumstances that had brought me here. It was the time of World War II, and I was a doctor. Instead of healing a Nazi general as I was supposed to do, I had poisoned and killed him. That was why these men were after me—they were seeking revenge.

In the next scene, I was looking down from above. I saw myself being strapped into an electric chair, and I watched as I was executed. I felt no pain; I was simply observing.

Then something truly beautiful happened. I watched my spirit rise from my body and drift slowly upward. It seemed to be following a trail of white light. At the end of that path there was an open door, through which the magnificent white light was streaming. At the door there stood a being that glowed with love and light, and it was waiting to greet my spirit. I felt such peace and love. I had a sense of being eternal.

"What lessons did you have to learn?" I heard my voice ask on the recording. I began to cry as I felt the simplicity and the profound truth of the lesson: be good; be loving.

That evening, I eagerly waited for my mother to return home from work. I told her what I had experienced. Being so young, I felt like the 1940s were times of antiquity, so I asked her whether electric chairs really existed during World War II. She said they did. I never felt the need to research the validity of the story any further. It felt so emotional, so real, that I never questioned it. I did not need proof to trust what I had experienced.

I find it interesting that this regression took place when I was 13. Mystics believe that the number 13 is the number of change and transformation. The number calls for a study of one's foundational beliefs and allows for changes in how a person de-fines everything in life, which is said to lead to shifts in a person's worldview and entire existence.

There is no doubt that my first regression had a tremendous impact on my life. The need to be good and loving became of par-amount importance to me. It colored my every step, every choice, and every conversation. It even made me realize how appropriate-ly my parents had named me. My full first name is Dobromira, which is a Slavic name composed of two words: *dobro,* meaning "good," and *mir,* meaning "peace, world." Following my regression, I chose to be someone who brings good into the world.

The Story Continues . . .

The story of my Nazi lifetime developed even further many years later, when I was at a workshop led by Brian Weiss. During one of the group regressions we did, an image of a long road lined with birch trees emerged in my mind. I saw myself as a young woman, walking down this quiet dirt road in the country. In my hand I carried a small suitcase, and on my head I had a kerchief. I was leaving my village to move to St. Petersburg to study medi-cine. The final stop I made on my way was at the cemetery, where I paid my respects at the graves of my dead relatives. My heart was heavy. I knew it might be many years before I would return back home—if ever.

While studying at the university, I was recruited by the secret service of the Soviet Union. There were troubles brewing in Europe, and even talks of a possible war. I was sent to Europe to spy for my country. As an attractive woman who knew how to use her charm, I found it very easy to gather information. I saw a vivid scene of me sitting in front of a small device, entering coded mes-sages to be sent back to the Soviet Union.

There was a nightclub that was frequented by many Ameri-cans, and I found myself going there as often as I could, hoping to meet a particular man I had come to know. I was surprised to discover that I was interested in him not for work, but because I was falling in love with him. He was in love with me, too.

The next scene unfolded on a large set of stairs in front of a big administrative building. I had received orders that I would be moving to a different location in Europe, so I had come to say good-bye to this man I loved. He begged me not to leave and asked me to marry him. Even though I wanted to very much, I could not stay. I had already given my word and pledged my life, my love, and my heart to my country. I assured him that when he went back home to his family farm in America he would marry a nice woman, have children, and be very happy. But my heart was breaking. I said good-bye, and with tears in my eyes I rushed down the stairs toward the car that was waiting for me.

Later, I married an important Nazi officer, which greatly facilitated my work and brought me protection. World War II had begun and I had been practicing medicine, mostly treating Nazi military men. I received orders to eliminate a high-ranking Nazi general whom I was treating for an illness. I saw myself standing in front of a table with a glass of water on it, and I was holding a small container of powder. The general was sitting on a chair next to me. I looked up toward the ceiling and, for a second that felt like an eternity, I experienced intense uncertainty about what I was getting ready to do. Yet thinking that I had no other choice, I poured the powder into the glass. Instead of giving the general his medication, I gave him poison.

This is where my first regression as a child fit in. I saw myself once again running down that hallway and eventually getting caught. Because I was much older and much better equipped to handle the painful scenes of the story, my Higher Self allowed me to see the gruesome details of the interrogations I was subjected to. Did I betray my network? No. Until the very end I maintained that I had acted alone. Over and over I was beaten, tortured, questioned, and then beaten, tortured, and questioned again. The only way my interrogators spared me was that they did not rape me. Because I was married to a Nazi officer, they felt that was a line they could not cross. In the end, as I had seen so long ago, they placed me in an electric chair and executed me.

As my spirit was rising above the scene, I once again knew that the lesson of that lifetime was of love—of needing to approach every situation with love and allowing myself to be loved, too. I knew that the entire lifetime had been orchestrated so that I could have the opportunity to choose love when standing on those stairs, to say yes when the American soldier asked me to marry him. Instead, I chose to stay true to my promise to serve my country. After I left, the soldier felt he had nothing to live for; my leaving had broken his spirit. I saw that he died in a dirt ditch, having been shot in the forehead during combat with the Nazi army.

In the hours that followed this regression I was shaken to my core. I was filled with an enormous sense of regret that my soul counterpart, the doctor, had harmed another human being. She knew that poisoning the general was wrong, yet she was caught in her limited perception of duty and obligation. She felt cornered by circumstances, and as a result, she did something that was against her instincts. Yet, knowing that we are eternal, I reminded myself that every lifetime enriches our soul with invaluable lessons. Knowing that I can—and that I prefer to—act with integrity, that I prefer not to harm others, is certainly a very valuable lesson.

Still, I deeply regretted that my counterpart had missed knowing love. It was clear to me that all the events that had taken place since she had arrived in Europe were meant to lead to that one moment on the stairs where she could choose love. I felt like she had wasted a whole lifetime. She ran away from love, and from herself, because she had vowed to serve her country selflessly.

Reflecting on the experience, I felt immense gratitude for the love that I know as the person I am today. My soul must have chosen to experience and learn the lesson of love in my current lifetime, because nothing gives me a greater sense of meaning and fulfillment than creating situations that are filled with love, light, and inspiration. One of the ways I most enjoy doing this is by helping others experience their other lives and gain understanding about the people and circumstances that surround them. And in my personal life I have been blessed with a loving relationship with a man who has two deep-seated and irrational fears. The first is a fear of losing me, and the second is a fear of being shot point-blank in the forehead.

Just the other day, my partner asked me, "Have you seen me in any of your past lives?" I said yes and reminded him of the life of the Russian spy. I realized I had never told him the vision I'd had of his death—of how, during the regression, I'd seen him crouched in a ditch. He'd popped up to shoot at the enemy, and had gotten shot in the forehead. After listening to me tell this story, he told me about a recurring dream he'd had many years before he'd met me.

"It was a very vivid dream that I clearly remember to this day. I was in a fight and got shot. I was lying in a ditch. There were others around me who were killed, some of them piled on me. Enemy soldiers were walking around looking for people who were still alive and shooting them. I tried to pretend that I was dead so that they wouldn't shoot me. But they found me, sensed that I was alive, and shot me."

We both looked at each other, feeling the deep connection between us. The Russian woman that I am in another life had given herself a second chance at love with the American soldier she once knew.

Parallel Realities of Possible Selves

Back at Brian Weiss's workshop, when he led our group into another regression, I easily slipped into the experience. I saw myself as the same Russian woman who had studied to become a doctor and was recruited to become a spy. I was sitting in a waiting room at a small airport. I knew I was a stewardess. *How could this be?* my mind protested. *I thought I had established what this life was about!*

I was dressed in a blue uniform. My fellow flight attendants were standing nearby, speaking Russian to each other. In my mind I was hearing and understanding the mundane conversation they were having. We boarded the plane and began performing our duties. The passengers were all government-level officials. I was serving drinks and handed a glass with vodka to Joseph Stalin, and I felt repulsion toward him. He was a brute, crude man with thick fingers. I went to the cockpit to offer the pilots a drink. The pilot who was the second in command had blond hair and blue eyes. His name was Serioja, and he was my fiancé. I loved him deeply and was excited about marrying him, having children, and sharing my life with him.

My mind couldn't understand what was going on. I questioned, *Wasn't I, as this woman, a spy? What happened?* I immediately knew that when the woman was offered the opportunity to be sent on a mission to Europe she declined. As a result, she was later assigned to be on the staff of Stalin's flight crew. A feeling of dissatisfaction persisted throughout her life. She always wondered whether she would have been better able to serve her beloved motherland had she taken that mission to go to Europe.

I came out of this regression feeling completely confused. I had no idea what had happened. In fact, for many years I chose to ignore this variation of the story. When sharing about the life of the Russian woman I would only tell people about the spy path of her life. The stewardess piece was sitting covered in dust in the back of my mind, waiting to be unwrapped and deliver its gifts.

What I had experienced was two possible lives of the same person, existing simultaneously. At the moment the Russian woman was presented with the choice of whether to go on a mission to Europe, her reality split into at least two different paths: the first was a life in which she took the mission, and the second was a life in which she declined it. You can see how this split would create two completely different lives—and these split realities would allow me to experience two completely different versions of her life during the regressions. I also imagine that there are parallel realities existing simultaneously with the two already mentioned in which she is never given this opportunity and her life developed on yet another path.

Each one of us has multiple "possible selves" existing right now. It's easy to imagine latent potentials that could be explored in the future. But there are roads not yet taken in your past as well. There are possible selves in your past waiting to emerge right now. Remember, the past is not done and complete. It is just another time stream. It is being created right now.

You can visualize this by picturing a decision tree. Whenever a choice is presented, our consciousness splits and experiences all possible variations of each situation. Each parallel self continues to create experiences and branch out into multiple possibilities. This applies to important decisions, such as whether to go to a specific college or whether to marry the person you're dating. It also applies to simple, everyday choices, such as whether to have a cup of coffee in the morning or take a different route on your way to work.

The very first time I came across the idea of the parallel existence of possible selves, I had a deep, intuitive understanding of it. It was clear to me that a creator, be it God or an Oversoul, would not want to be limited to experiencing life on one singular track. Were it so, this mighty power would be severely underutilizing its abilities; it would not be fulfilling its creative impulse to be in a constant state of becoming more. I know you too will easily and intuitively understand the idea of how exploring different possibilities creates parallel realities.

A Scientific Explanation

Allow me now to speak to your rational, logical mind and offer you a scientific explanation for the parallel existence of your possible lives. In 1954, a brilliant man by the name of Hugh Everett III formulated a quantum-physics theory that describes the concept of parallel universes. At the time of its introduction, this theory was considered radical and was rather fervently rejected by established physicists. Today it is very much in use in different fields of science and technology and is widely acknowledged.

Simply put, the "many worlds" theory states that everything that is possible happens. Each event splits into different realities and the observer, or the person existing within the event, also splits as his or her world does. In the moment that an event is observed, the act of observation creates the event and creates a split in which all possible variations of the event are formed into a parallel reality, each having its own version of the observer.

Recently, scientists have proven that the rules governing the world of quantum particles also apply to human-size objects. Quantum physicist Aaron O'Connell created an object visible to the naked eye that can be shown to be both vibrating and not vibrating at the same time. This means that the object is in two different places at the same time. Such a state of dual existence has previously been proven only with quantum particles.

Your soul is creating with every choice you make. You are constantly faced with new realities, new "yous" that are exploring all the possibilities. Your soul is not limited by time, and because of that a new possibility can be born in any moment—in your past, present, or future.

The versions of your reality that you are not consciously aware of—that you are not "observing" right now—exist on a different vibrational level. Each contains its own version of "you." Those other versions of you experience their worlds in as real a way as you experience your own reality. They share the same personal history as the self you are aware of, up until the moment of the split in consciousness. At that moment, you and your other self each took on a different set of possibilities, based on the choice you made.

Yet a new past can also be born in any moment, and your experience of it will be so natural and seamless that you may not even notice. Without realizing it, you will shift to a different reality where you always had that past as part of your history.

Kalila's Story

I want to share with you an example of how, in every moment, we can allow for a new possibility. We can always choose differently to create our best possible life. Kalila's story clearly exemplifies how a single moment of choice creates a split in our reality.

Kalila's parents had had her when they were very young. They thought that they would not be able to raise her properly, so they sent her to a boarding school. She was a good student and had a lot of friends, but she didn't like all the rules she had to follow at the school. Eventually, she went on to become a successful lawyer. She worked a lot—once again, following the rules. Later she got married and had kids, and she was relatively happy. But she still felt a sense of regret. When I asked her why, she replied:

> *Kalila:* I wanted to do something more expressive, without time and rules. Like dancing. I wanted to dance. I wanted to be onstage. But I didn't even know that until later on. By then I had already been married and had kids, and had to follow even more rules because I had to feed them and get them to school. . . . I lived a happy life, and had a great family. It's just that there was always something inside of me, a little spark of something, that wished it could have expressed itself a little more. But I was still pretty happy.

I feel very guided during my work with clients, and with Kalila my instincts told me that it would serve her to explore a different version of her life. I had her go back to the moment when she was sensing within her that there was something else that could have made her happier. I wanted her to see how a life where she had completely fulfilled that creative calling would have played out:

> *Kalila:* I start to take dance lessons. I get a singing coach.

> *Mira:* Are you still a lawyer or did you decide not to study law?

Kalila: I decided not to go. There is a gap in time where I chose not to go, even though I had the opportunity. I decided to take the other fork in the road. I practice a lot. I took the lessons I wanted to take. I got to do these shows where I'd go onstage and perform all the things that I practiced and just express myself. It felt so good because I didn't plan everything out, I just kind of expressed myself. It felt right. I didn't have to figure anything out. I just knew that this is the way my body was supposed to go or these are the words I was going to sing. It felt so good to know that I could just get onstage and trust. I enjoyed practice because it was a way to express my inner self and my joy for life. So when it came time to perform it just felt the same. It was nice because people enjoyed my performances. They liked that I could just be myself. They were happy that I was willing to express what I was feeling in the moment.

Mira: Wonderful. Do you meet someone and have a family?

Kalila: I meet somebody. We travel a lot, though. We go and explore other places. He is very expressive, too. He knows how to express himself. And he is so gentle. Eventually we have a family, but first we go and experience new things. Things I always wanted to do.

Mira: So this is a good relationship for you?

Kalila: Yeah. I didn't think there could be one like that. I feel like I had no idea what . . . it's like it is the first time I actually had a relationship. I didn't know one could be like that.

I asked Kalila to look at the two versions of that life and tell me whether she had the same partner or whether they were two different people. She said her husbands were two different people. One was more restrictive, the way she was with her own life. The other was much more open and flowing and allowing. But that was only because she chose a different path, she told me. When she did that for herself, she was able to have somebody who matched that in her. We continued:

Mira: What did the two versions of the same life serve you to understand?

Kalila: The biggest thing that it served me to understand is that I am allowing. I am a piece of allowing. The purpose was to walk through life and allow, and listen. All possibilities are there. They are available. To experience every moment and just be. In the other version, I picked up on all this stuff about the rules, so I kept following the rules. I attracted somebody else who was doing what they were taught to, and we passed that on to our kids. The lesson of allowing made all the difference in the world. I first made the change because I was listening, and I allowed a piece of advice to take me to a different place.

Mira: What was different in the moment when you listened to yourself?

Kalila: It was just a space of letting go and listening. In the other version I was doing what I was supposed to be doing, but all the doing got in my way. If I had stopped doing and allowed more, I would have heard what was meant to happen next.

In that moment of listening and allowing, Kalila became a different person. She perceived new possibilities for herself and expanded her beliefs about what was possible for her. Simply by doing that, she embarked on a new possible life.

Becoming a Different Person

Quantum physics tells us that every moment is a new moment. It teaches us that there is no continuity between events, that each event is a separate occurrence. Yet our minds are masterful at creating flow—manufacturing causality and continuity between events. Because we are not equipped to experience multiple realities, we feel that our life naturally progresses on a singular track.

The ability to shift between possibilities—to constantly allow for change in our lives—is so innate that we do not usually notice that we have changed into a new person. When we shift to a new possible reality, it usually seems that we simply made a choice. It seems that we have always been the person who would have made that choice. We look back to our past and can point to events that have seemingly caused us to become exactly who we are in this moment. But in reality, our beliefs, thoughts, and expectations of what was possible got us to where we are today. They align us with the reality of the vibrationally matching possibility.

I clearly remember one evening having dinner with friends and talking about parallel realities. It had been a year since I'd decided to no longer pursue my legal career and insteaed dedicate myself to my love of spirituality. Sitting at the dinner table, I observed myself. I recognized that my identity as a regressionist felt very strong. Not only that, but I felt as though my previous life as an attorney had never existed. I, as the regressionist, felt as if I had never been a corporate lawyer at all. I even looked back to my childhood and was able to list all the events that had pointed in the direction of my new career. It seemed as though I would inevitably be a regressionist one day.

We gracefully flow from one possibility into another, blending them seamlessly. Each possibility we choose creates a past from which the present logically seems to have followed. So it seems to me that I have *always* been a regressionist, so much so that it seems unreal to think I was ever a lawyer.

The shift between different possibilities is usually subtle for the one who experiences it. Yet those around that person always notice the change. We've all had those moments when we've encountered people we used to know and something about them seems different. We don't know what it is, exactly, but we immediately pick up on a new energy. Recently, I saw a friend I had not seen in a few months. She casually asked me, "Something is different about you. Is it your hair?" Yes, my hair had grown a bit since she had seen me last, but what she was actually picking up on was a whole lot of emotional healing and releasing that I had just been through. That inner work had allowed me to shift to a greater level of expansion and new possible realities, and she could feel it.

There are also times when we undergo major changes—a new job, the end of a relationship, and so on—and we attribute such changes to forks in the road of life, when in fact they are reality shifts. Such events are few and far and between, however. More often, the shifts between realities are subtle—so subtle we may not even notice them.

○

Your soul desires new opportunities for growth, so it seeks to create new avenues for the expression of its creative energy. Your myriad possible selves allow this desire to become reality.

All of your present experiences are drawn from what was once a possible reality. There is an inexhaustible array of possibilities you could pick from to shift in the direction of growth and expansion. So how is it, then, that you choose one specific possibility as opposed to another? The answer is simple: beliefs create reality.

Your beliefs about who you are define what is possible and what is not possible for you. Your beliefs act as a filter, which allows into awareness only the possibilities that are in line with your self-image. As I said earlier, our brains process 400 billion bits of information per second, but only 2,000 bits register in our awareness.

There are endless possible realities. Every situation has countless possible ways to manifest. In one reality or another, all of these possibilities are experienced. But your consciousness will choose from this infinite field of potential only the paths that are in accord with who you believe yourself to be. As a result, when you change the idea of who you are, your life experience changes as well. Space opens up for new possibilities.

The physical state of your body also follows your beliefs. In his book *The Biology of Belief,* Dr. Bruce Lipton discusses the connection between cell biology and quantum physics. He shows that the way our DNA is expressed is controlled by the positive and negative energetic messages of our thoughts. The moment we alter the messages we send our cells, our DNA adjusts accordingly.

One of the most valuable aspects of regression is that it allows people to transform their beliefs. When people transform their beliefs about their personality, abilities, body, and relationships, their experience of life changes. For example, I had a session with a woman whose adult children arranged for us to meet. She came into my office and very politely told me that she did not believe that what I do could help her, but she showed up to appease her children. After all, years in therapy had not changed things. How could a single session with me help? Eighteen years after the end of her marriage, she was still filled with negative emotions that were hampering her life, her ability to be in new relationships, and her health.

Needless to say, we had a very profound and deeply moving session. At the end of our time together, after I brought her back to normal consciousness, I asked how she felt. She opened her eyes and looked at me with the look of a person for whom everything has changed in a moment. "I feel transformed," she said. "I feel like a new person."

She was right. She was no longer the same person she had been before our time together. Her experience of other lives had altered her beliefs about herself, her love life, and her health. The world for her had changed. I encouraged her to trust that the change would be permanent, and to fully behave as the person she now was.

How to Consciously Choose New Possibilities

Each of the events of our lives was once only a possibility. Our choices brought the events forth from the infinite field of possibilities into physical materialization. It's easy to think of possibilities as potentials to be developed in the future. It's much harder to consider that we might have potentials available in the past, waiting to be expressed. But it's true! Because past, present, and future all exist simultaneously, there are latent potentials available in the past awaiting to be expressed. New situations, abilities, and states of health can be created in the present—resulting in a new past, right now. Because of the way our consciousness flows through possibilities and creates continuity, we are rarely able to perceive the creation of new possibilities in the past. Yet this mechanism of reality creation is part of the nature of existence. I want to acquaint you with it so you use it in the creation of your best life yet.

The present moment is the only moment through which you create your life. It is in the present where you have the power to reach into both the past and the future, creating the change you desire. When a belief you hold is altered in the present, you are able to create changes in your cellular structure and your energy field as they existed in the past. The release of emotional issues and negative beliefs in the present will affect the past. Your old psychological essence and biological makeup, as they existed at a specific point in the past, are altered. As a result, the conditions are released in the present, but also a new past is created. In the present moment you choose a new past. In this new past, you never experienced those conditions, or you experienced them in a much milder form.

If these ideas are new and hard to assimilate, let me present them through the understanding of cause and effect. If something is different about you in the present moment, the cause could only be a change that happened in the past. Only a specific past could cause a certain present. When you change in the present, that change automatically comes with a new past—because only *that* past could have brought the new present.

An example is a new and intense belief in health and well-being. Such a belief would create new ideas of health and vitality that would be absorbed by the cells in the past. Because everything is happening simultaneously, any change in the present will necessarily affect both the past and the future. It's as if the old cellular memories are taken out and new ones are inserted. A new possibility of well-being is born in the past, and it becomes our history. Our cells in the present start to mirror our attitude about health and vitality. We respond to this belief environment by choosing a new reality of health, rather than sickness. We are rarely consciously aware of such a shift, so when we experience a resurgence of health in the present moment we often call the healing a "miracle." But in fact, it's a testament to the power we have to create our lives in the present moment.

The same approach can be applied to abilities you may consider dormant. Think of all the skills and talents that you have that aren't well developed—each represents a possibility to be actualized. When activated, these new avenues of expression and creativity can enrich your life in satisfying ways. To bring them into your experience, simply choose to have those talents become part of your life and identity. Think about these skills in your daily life, and use your imagination and focus upon the ways in which they bring you joy. Your attention and intention actualize a past where those experiences become a part of your life. As a result, you respond differently to memories from the past. You create a future where you become a person who has that new past as part of your identity.

How we remember new moments from our past differs for everyone. Some of us experience it so seamlessly that it is as if our new attitudes have always been there. Others create a more jarring recognition—actually remembering two different versions of the past—or construct new memories of the past that we are *aware* are new. Each one of us has our own reasons for the different ways we are aware of our power to create.

Reprogramming the Past

During the process of writing this book, it became very clear to me that my written words were constantly being mirrored or actualized in one way or another in my daily reality. It was no surprise, then, that while writing about awakening dormant talents I was able to apply the process itself. This is a story about water.

Growing up, my experiences with water included the occasional seaside vacation and a three-month-long swimming class when I was seven years old. I learned the swimming techniques, but I never excelled. I enjoyed getting in the water when the rare opportunity presented itself, but swimming never seemed appealing to me, especially when it came to the ocean. The destructive power and force of the waves scared me. It also scared me that, unlike a swimming pool, I could not see what was around me when I was in the ocean. These two fears combined to create the feeling that the ocean was not a natural environment for me.

All this was bound to rise to the surface when I went to live on Maui. Because of my "healthy" fears and my lack of excitement for the ocean, it took me two full weeks before I decided to get in the water. As I was getting in, I did my mandatory dance—moving slowly and shivering from the cold. While treading in the water, I sent out awareness in all directions to act as a radar. I was scared some sea creature would come close to me, scare me, or even bite me. Just as I began encouraging myself that I was doing really well and was safe, I felt something enter my personal space. I couldn't see anything, so again I reminded myself that I was safe. A moment later, a woman who was snorkeling behind me came up out of the water and with great enthusiasm yelled, "There is a big turtle right underneath you!" I dashed for the shore in a state of sheer panic. Not being a great swimmer, I couldn't move particularly fast, which panicked me even more. A part of me said, "Mira, it is just a turtle. It's not going to harm you." Yet all I wanted was to get to the beach.

When I got to the shore I took a breath of relief. Guess what I did next? I went back to the edge of the water to look at the turtle! I had never seen one before, and now that I was safe on dry land, I was curious! I couldn't help but laugh at myself. Literally, I laughed out loud. At that moment I decided that my attitude toward the ocean needed to change.

I thought of the swimming skills that lay dormant in my field of potentiality. I chose to allow the potential of me as a swimmer to expand and take hold. Because imagination coupled with an intense desire creates new realities, I imagined what it would have been like if I had continued swimming regularly after that class I'd taken when I was little. I allowed myself to think of myself as a person who had a different past—one where she swam often and well. I began to act like someone who is the result of that different past. I imagined myself as a little girl, continuing to swim every chance I got. I imagined how my past could have been different had swimming been part of it. I imagined joining a swim team and going to competitions. I imagined always having loved being in the water.

Whenever I got back in the ocean, I'd send love and thoughts of harmonious coexistence to all creatures. In my mind I spoke to the ocean and thanked it for loving me and always taking care of me; this allowed me to feel safe and protected. Suddenly, I could not wait to get in the water. I would plunge right in rather than make it a slow and painful entry. I bought snorkeling gear so I could see how beautiful the ocean environment was. I began thinking of myself as someone who knows how to swim well. When moving my arms and legs, I imagined I had good form. I started tuning in to swimming events being broadcast on TV. In every possible way my imagination and thoughts focused on my self-image as a person who loves to swim.

All this allowed me to see myself in a new light. It created such an area of joy and expansion for me that I looked forward to my time in the water. The power of the waves no longer intimidated me. Instead, I saw them as a creative force with which I could merge my own energy and creative essence. In those moments I experience exalting, exuberant joy and the awareness of my own power. I no longer worried about not being able to see what was around me; I knew I was safe and at home in the water. I started thinking of my swimming past in a different light and experienced a different effect in the present. My new belief about being a swimmer reprogrammed my past and provided me with an experience that has enriched my present.

Remind yourself that beliefs are nothing more than assumptions you have accepted as truths. Once you have brought those beliefs to the surface and seen them simply as thoughts that can easily be changed, you are already on your way to changing your reality.

Your path in life is not settled. Your experience is simply a reflection of the beliefs you hold about what is possible for you.

There are infinite possible actions available, infinite possible realities you can shift to. Whatever you desire, there is a possible reality in which you're getting just what you want—wealth, close friends, good health, a comfortable home, loving partnerships, and so on. There is a possible "you" who experiences all of those blessings; it's simply a matter of merging your consciousness with that possibility.

Exercise: How to Shift into the Reality You Prefer

This exercise is meant to shift you into a parallel reality where you can experience a life of desirable possibilities. There are two parts to this exercise. The first one asks you to set aside some quiet time and explore through journaling. The second part is an ongoing practice.

1. Set aside 30 minutes and sit somewhere quiet with your journal nearby. Begin by dedicating the next few moments to diving within. Think of a situation in your life that you want to transform. Knowing that beliefs are the master plan used to create your reality, look at the core thoughts that are the kernels of your present situation. Remember, a belief is simply a thought—a point of view you hold as the truth. Ask yourself what thoughts you would have to hold as truths for this situation to be as it is. Write down the beliefs you have about your circumstances. You will notice that a couple will stand out as your core beliefs, as the repetitive and most emotional thoughts on the matter. It will seem as if all other beliefs can be explained through these one or two core beliefs. The rest of the thoughts you list will be beliefs that have branched off the core beliefs.

Let's use the example of a man who is lonely. He is successful in his career, yet in his personal life he feels completely alone. He had a traumatic childhood, and his intimate relationships have been difficult. At first his list will be focused on the external. It may say: *It is hard to make friends; everyone is busy with their life.* Then he may go into his history: *I was never loved as a child; as a little boy I was innocent and open, and they hurt me. I am afraid to trust; life experiences keep on confirming for me that it is not safe to let people in.* The emotions will rise, but if he stays with it he will inevitably get to the core of it all: *I am not lovable; if I were lovable, my mom would have loved me. I am afraid to let people in because if they truly know who I am, they too will leave.* At its core, his loneliness issue has nothing to do with his friends or ability to be social but with his feeling of unworthiness and not deserving love.

Once you have identified your core assumption, ask yourself what beliefs you would have to hold in order to have a preferable experience. Transform each of the limiting beliefs you wrote down into a belief that would support what you desire. Write down those new positive beliefs.

In our example it would be as follows: *I am worthy. There are so many wonderful things about me. My coming into the world is not an accident of procreation. My very existence is proof that I am worthy; otherwise, God would not have created me. My mom's inability to love and nurture me was not caused by me. She had her own challenges and issues that had nothing to do with me. The partners who left did not leave because I was not lovable, but because it was right for us to separate; our paths were diverging. I was keeping people at a distance, so I was attracting friends who were comfortable with that. I am a good, loyal, and reliable person; it is safe to let people see that about me. It is safe to communicate and open up to people. I am worthy of feeling unity with others. I am worthy of feeling loved.*

2. The next part is an ongoing practice that you will be repeating in the days to come. Set your notebook aside. Close your eyes and take a deep breath. Before you begin this session of reprogramming your past, present, and future, remind yourself that in this moment you hold the power to shift and create a new reality for yourself. Then, imagine the events you desire. Imagine them in vivid pictures. Bring in all of your senses—how would it feel, sound, smell, taste, and look for you to be getting exactly what you want? In your mind repeat the new beliefs you are adopting. And most important, feel—deeply and intensely—the joy, love, fulfillment, and satisfaction you would get from this new life.

In our example, the man would think of ways to communicate more with the world. He would imagine what it would feel like to sense connection with everyone. He would imagine having many friends, and the ways they would interact and spend time together. He would imagine feeling appreciated and loved. He would imagine opening up to a perfect partner and what their relationship would be like.

Dedicate five to ten minutes once or twice a day to imagining the new possible events taking place in your life. Make it a special and enjoyable time for yourself each day. Soon you will begin to notice the world around you showing signs of change. The situation will change, because you have changed.

Anchoring Your New Reality

We are only able to imagine new possibilities because they already exist as a reality somewhere. Our intention and the intensity of our desire fuel the shift into that reality. Each of us is just one possible version of ourselves; there are many other possible versions. By changing our beliefs, we refocus and become the version we desire.

There's one very important idea to remember, so please take note: *What you desire and what you presently have are two separate realities.* Do not fight what you have or attempt to change it. You don't even need to pretend that you're ignoring it—be at peace with it. See it as a confirmation of your ability to flawlessly align with realities that reflect your beliefs.

There is no conflict between the preferred and nonpreferred events. The undesired aspect is simply one possible reality that you have materialized. Every possible reality is the reflection of a specific idea or belief. You can think of it as a static snapshot. In every specific reality there is no room for the expression of any other beliefs. Each reality is a single frame capturing a single idea. Change comes because you change *yourself.* You change your perspective and your thoughts on a given subject. By doing so, you shift to a new reality.

In those preferred and undesired realities, there are two different versions of you. Ask yourself, "How am I different in the reality where I have what I want?" See that version of you in your daily life. How are you feeling? How are you relating to the people around you? How are you doing the chores of daily life? Then, begin to *act like* that version of you. This final step anchors the reality-creation process. By acting on the new beliefs as the preferred you, you are telling yourself and the Universe that you are at the helm of your life and that you have the trust, knowingness, faith, vision, and power to call in from the infinite field of potential the life you desire the most.

How quickly will the life that you desire manifest? The speed of reality transformation depends on how quickly you can change your beliefs. As you will see in the story of Anita Moorjani in Chapter 7, when beliefs are changed instantaneously, very little time is required for the structure of reality to morph to fit the new situation. Any time delay is the result of the physical structure of the world and the neurological structure of our bodies. A small car doesn't need much time to accelerate from a complete stop to a very high speed, or to go from a fast speed to a complete stop. Similarly, in the realm of Spirit, where the physicality is of a lesser density, manifestation is immediate. But on Earth, it's like we're driving a big, heavy truck. Because things are so much denser here, there is a delay between a change in belief and its actualization into matter.

First we must stop the momentum our prior thoughts have created. Then we need to give our neurons time to adjust to the way they pick up data from the environment. New possibilities must be awakened in the past before we can experience the benefits and results of them today. Knowing this, all you have to do is trust the process. The world will reflect your changed convictions.

Nothing about your personality is a permanent construct. You are constantly changing; with every new choice you make, you experience yourself as a new person. You are constantly shifting between parallel universes. These universes, these snapshots of certain circumstances, all exist in the present moment. It is through your choices in every single situation that you become the vibration of one or another parallel life that you experience as your reality.

We create the past by remembering events and interpreting them in a way that gives us the effect we are seeking in the present. Now that this expanded perspective has been planted in you, you can begin to play with it. The more you see the situations in your life through this new prism, the more you will find yourself living an ever-expanding life filled with awe, synchronicities, and magic. I know it to be true, because that is what has happened for me.

I love to say how my life is an ecstatic explosion of synchronicities. An important part of that love for my life has been my connection with my Higher Self. Becoming aware of my Higher Self, and strengthening my communication with that part of me, has allowed me to find a deeper sense of trust in myself and in the development of my life. In the chapter that follows I will share with you how I guide people to connect with their own Higher Self during regression, and how you can do the same to receive guidance, nurturance, healing, and assurance.

CHAPTER 4

YOU CAN CONVERSE WITH YOUR HIGHER SELF

Each one of us has a *Higher Self,* which is a term I like to use to refer to the wise and unconditionally loving part of ourselves. The Higher Self holds the template of our greatest potential. It represents the greatest possible manifestation of certain themes and goals our soul would like to explore in this life. It is the highest possible evolution our soul would like to create through our human life. It's part of us, the vibration of our true self. And it's always here, ready to connect with us.

When we're not aware of our unity with all and our connection with the Divine, our ego feels alone. It feels as if it is carrying the world on its shoulders, and that it needs to figure everything out. We get into these frenzied mental states, desperately needing to come up with a solution. Because we are disconnected from our Higher Self, from our guidance system, we really feel lost. We feel unsupported in everyday decisions and unable to see the bigger picture and meaning of our lives.

Almost every client who comes to me has the same question: "What is my purpose?" It is the very mission of our Higher Self to guide us to the fulfillment of this potential. Because of that, our

Higher Self is tirelessly orchestrating circumstances for us, while communicating with and guiding us. Our mind can choose to trust the Higher Self, to check in and listen, or it can choose to ignore the signals. The Higher Self will do everything it can to have us fulfill our plan for this life. So why do we resist it? Why do we ignore it to the point that it has to use accidents and abrupt changes to get us back on our soul's path?

My regression work has taught me that the ego and the Higher Self are meant to work together as one. This is one of the reasons why regression sessions are so transformative and my clients leave profoundly affected by the experience—because they welcome *all of* who they are home. They feel whole and complete. They feel connected. They feel guided and supported, with clear direction on how to proceed. They receive emotional and physical healing. They allow for their beliefs and mental limitations to transform. But best of all, they feel love—the unconditional love of Source for who they are.

People often wonder how the presence of the Higher Self feels to the regressed person. Here is what John says: "When I think back to our session, I always struggled to explain how it felt when you were talking to my 'higher' self. In the preface to *Seth, Dreams and Projections of Consciousness*, Jane Roberts talks about how it feels when Seth comes through. She couldn't have explained it better. She says, 'It is not a neutral energy but one of strong emotional impact, reassuring, and in an odd way, personified—warm and amazingly immediate. Perhaps it envelops me, but I do not fall asleep or lose myself in nothingness. I am myself, but very small. I seem to fade into a distance that has nothing to do with space but more to do with psychological focus. Yet I am upheld, supported and protected in the midst of this pervading energy that seems to form about and within me.' The part about feeling small and fading into space is exactly how I felt during the session."

This is how John experienced connecting with his Higher Self, but everyone experiences it differently. Some people describe the experience just like John and Jane Roberts do. Others feel as if they step to the side—as if someone else is speaking through them, even though they are still fully conscious. They don't assign value to what is being spoken; they simply give voice to the impulse within them. And only after they listen to the recording of the session do they hear and understand the words they uttered.

For others it feels as if nothing unusual is happening at all. The skies are not parting, and God is not speaking to them in a booming voice. They feel like themselves. When I ask questions, they feel that they are answering the questions themselves, from a deep place of inner knowing. Yet they feel expanded in their awareness, as if they are standing on a mountaintop and taking in the entire view—seeing the bigger picture and understanding all the connections. Often after listening to the recording of our session, such clients will e-mail me and ask, "Where did this come from? At the time I thought it was just me responding to your questions, but I am not that wise! I don't talk like that; I don't even think like that. My voice, my choice of words, my intonation, and my energy were all different."

This way of experiencing the Higher Self seems completely natural to me, because the Higher Self is part of us—the part of us that is not focused on physical reality. I assure every client that we are constantly guided, and we can trust how it unfolded. That's how the information was conveyed to them. The Higher Self always connects in ways that are appropriate to the client, and the guidance offered is perfectly attuned to what that person needs to grow and shift in that moment.

The Higher Self's Suggestion: Meditation

During his regression, John discovered that he had been reborn over and over again, in an attempt to learn the same lesson. By the time we'd investigated six different lives, he was feeling frustrated that he was not fully understanding the lesson he was meant to learn. I knew it was time to guide him into connecting with the energy of his Higher Self.

I instructed him to allow his energy to expand. Once the Higher Self indicated that it was present, I asked it why John had been presented with these six lifetimes as opposed to any others he might have seen. The Higher Self responded that these lives were chosen so he could see what was still missing: the lesson of understanding.

The Higher Self added, "He's doing very well this time. He's pretty much always focused on understanding. He understands other people's situations very well." I asked what he needed to understand about his *own* situation. The answer was simple: "To relax. He's always worried, thinking, *What about this, what about that.* All it takes is a little meditation." John's Higher Self recommended that he meditate before going to bed each night.

Meditation is a common recommendation I hear from the Higher Self, yet each time the suggestion is tailored to the client's particular needs. Here, for example, bedtime was indicated as better for John than any other time of day. But regardless of the specific suggestions, meditation is a valuable tool to clear the mind of busy and confusing energy and to check in with guidance and intuition. Recently, a client told me she needed to really learn how to meditate. My response was that meditation is not something you learn or a skill to be acquired. Meditation is something you already know; it's something you already *are.*

Within you there is a beautiful realm of peace, tranquility, trust, and understanding, and you naturally know how to attune to it. Close your eyes, take a deep, slow breath in, and slowly exhale. The moment you do that, a sense of calm is instantly upon you. You are there. It's important to change the thought from *I need to learn* to *I already know how.* Then meditating will no longer be something foreign that you shy away from—it will feel like coming home. Meditating will feel replenishing, like drinking from a well of pure love and light.

There are many meditation techniques to choose from. I recommend the guided meditation that is part of my CD set, *Healing Through Past-Life Regression . . . and Beyond*, but any technique will do. Trust your instincts to select an approach that is right for you.

The magic of meditation is not in the technique; it comes from you, from your willingness to be open, to trust and explore. What you will discover is always more of who you are.

Help from the Soul Group

A soul group is a community of souls who create close relationships with one another across different incarnations. They are forever there for each other, willing to play whatever roles are necessary to support each other in their mutual growth.

John had always felt very strongly connected with his grandfather, and I asked his Higher Self why that was the case. In the answer, John recognized the deep connection he had to his family members—how they all assist him in gaining understanding, the biggest lesson of his life:

> *John's Higher Self:* [John's grandfather] is another part of his soul group. We sent him back down [to Earth] because John was having so much trouble with the understanding part.
>
> *Mira:* So his grandfather came to help him?
>
> *John's Higher Self:* As a teacher, yes.
>
> *Mira:* How is he helping him?
>
> *John's Higher Self:* Learning to teach. Teaching to teach.
>
> *Mira:* How is the grandfather doing that?
>
> *John's Higher Self:* He is not doing anything. He is just being himself.

This was an important lesson for John—and for me. By simply being who we are, we affect the world in ways that no amount of "doing" could ever accomplish. We can be true to ourselves, knowing that we are already impacting those around us by shining our light with love, kindness, and understanding. This is what we can do to best help those in our soul group—we can simply be ourselves.

John's Higher Self went on to report that the thing standing in John's way was all his worry. Like all of us, John worried too much. When we spend all of our time in worry, we forget what we've come here to do.

As John's Higher Self explained, this was the very lesson John was here to teach others: how to become who we really are. John didn't need to master the skill before he started teaching, however. His Higher Self said, "You have to teach to understand." I love the wisdom in these words. I too have found this to be true. The more I share with people and the more I write about a certain idea, the deeper my understanding becomes.

Adopting the "teach to understand" approach as a conscious tool can help us further our own learning and growth, as well as that of our soul group. When faced with changes, we can meditate on the lessons. Every situation is there to serve us. We can seek to understand the benefits our challenges provide. Then it is up to us to share those ideas with others. The more we share, the greater our insight will become. Having to explain these concepts to others makes us go deeper, internalizing the meaning of the ideas. Does the method of sharing matter? No. It could be through a story, a song, a poem, a drawing, or even a simple comment extended to a stranger. What matters is that we give voice to the wisdom welling inside of us. We are all here to constantly inspire each other, and by doing that, to uplift ourselves.

This is what John's grandfather was doing for him. I asked John's Higher Self who else was part of John's soul group. His Higher Self named a couple of his close friends and everyone from his immediate family. When I jokingly said that this was a family that likes to travel together, the Higher Self agreed that "they don't separate too often." Through my own personal regressions and working with clients, I have come to learn that we often reincarnate with people we have known in other lives. We create patterns by interacting with each other in life, and then we choose to shift the pieces of the pattern a bit so we can learn from different perspectives.

And who better to assist us than the people with whom we initially created those patterns?

Our commitment to our soul group often determines our geographical location as well. I asked John's Higher Self whether he thought John should consider moving, and he said no. "The focus of his lesson is here and everyone is based here," John's Higher Self explained. "If he goes anywhere else, he wouldn't be able to teach the lesson of understanding to the people he needs to." John's soul group was primarily located in and around New York, so that was where he needed to stay.

I asked John's Higher Self why his friends and family were not as interested in spiritual topics as John was. The answer surprised me, yet it made sense. Because John's lesson in this life was to learn and teach understanding, it would not be appropriate if his friends and family were just as involved in metaphysical ideas as he was. If they were, he would not be able to teach them and learn through his interactions with them.

"They're not supposed to support him," the Higher Self explained. "He's supposed to support *them*." John simply needed to be comfortable with his beliefs and let go of the need for their affirmation or permission.

This is a good lesson for all of us. If you have a partner, children, or friends who don't share your passion for the spiritual, do not despair; perhaps they have mastered that area in another life. If so, it's no wonder they have no need to devour every New Age book you do, in a constant search for answers. Be comfortable with what you believe in; allow them to be supportive but not interested. There are always many other like-minded people with whom you can have tantalizing conversations about spiritual principles. You cannot change anyone. Stay in your own energy and give those around you your unconditional love. Who knows? Maybe they're members of your soul group, here to help you learn the lessons of love and understanding.

One more thing about John. When I asked his Higher Self whether he needed to focus on anything when meditating, the answer was, "Just himself." The answer seemed a bit cryptic, so I asked for a little help. The reply surprised me:

John's Higher Self: I'm only going to give him one hint.

Mira: What is it?

John's Higher Self: Jan is going to be there. Pretty soon. Sooner than he thinks. He shouldn't worry too much.

Mira: How will he recognize her?

John's Higher Self: He'll know.

Mira: Are they going to be mates again?

John's Higher Self: Yes. He'll marry her.

"Pretty soon" turned out to be an understatement. Not more than a week after our session, John met Jan. (In this life she goes by a different name, but to keep things simple I will continue to refer to her as Jan.) He e-mailed me a brief note saying, "As an FYI, I'm 100 percent sure I've met Jan—turns out we work together . . ." She happened to sit 60 feet away from him. At the time of his session, John had been new to the company and had yet to meet most of the people who worked there. Ten months later he proposed to her. Some of his friends expressed concern that it may be too soon, but John and I knew better. During our session John saw how their souls were created together.

Here is how he described it: "I can see this sphere of white light dropping down out of nowhere and it breaks off. We're stuck together. It's not like two separate pieces. The things inside don't even have a shape. We don't have a band connecting us. We're connected in a different way."

The connection John and Jan have is very special. They have been together since the moment of the creation of their souls. They have loved each other for all eternity. They have spent lifetimes together. And in this life they have chosen to be together again. Does that mean their relationship is perfect? Of course not. Like any other couple, they have challenges. But John understands their connection, and his love and dedication to Jan is awe inspiring.

John married Jan a year after they met, and they now have their first child together—a precious little boy who is himself probably here to teach John about understanding. John and Jan have not visited Paris together yet, but I know that when they do, they will have a great time.

Ivan's Story

Even though I seek to communicate with a client's Higher Self during sessions, I know that the consciousness I access is even greater. Our being stems from the One—the single source of all existence. We are all part of the one field of information. Therefore, the guidance and healing a client receives comes from the highest level of love and well-being that is appropriate for the person. It may originate from the souls who serve to guide the person while on Earth, from the person's soul group, from the energy consciousness of a spiritual brotherhood, or from the angelic realm or any other dimension of existence the person is connected to. No matter the source, the help is always extended with unconditional love and acceptance, and with the desire to further the person's path into the Light.

Because of the greater density of our earthly environment, we are accustomed to a relatively slow energy frequency. The frequency of the information and healing offered to a client is often outside the range compatible with that person's energy frequency. So that the guidance can be understood, the healing and answers are translated through the vibration of the person's Higher Self. Just like a quantum physicist would need to teach a five-year-old in a different way than he would teach his graduate students, so does All That Is put its guidance in a language and energy that is understandable and within range.

An example of this took place during my session with a client named Ivan. Before our regression began, we spoke about the questions he wanted to have answered by his Higher Self. He wanted to know whom his guardian angel was and how to communicate with him or her. I diligently wrote the question down. At one point during the conversation with the Higher Self, I glanced at my notes and saw the question on the guardian angel. A burst of intuition told me that I needed to ask for Ivan to *see* the angel, rather than just receiving a name. I trusted the impulse without questioning it and addressed the Higher Self, asking for the angel to reveal itself to Ivan. To my surprise, the angel began speaking *through* Ivan, introducing himself directly as the angel Damian.

It was breathtaking to notice how different the delivery was when the words were coming from the angel rather than Ivan himself. His voice changed, and the words were spoken with authority and intensity. The energy coming through Ivan completely changed in that moment, because a different being was speaking. Just as quickly, the angel was gone and Ivan's voice was soft and relaxed once again. I wanted to know more about the angel, however, so I continued the conversation:

Mira: Give me a description of what you saw as Angel Damian came forward.

Ivan's Higher Self: From the light this person with a white robe, a light halo around his head and wings, and holding some kind of piece of stick stepped out.

Mira: Ask Angel Damian how to communicate with him.

Ivan's Higher Self: He says, "You already communicate with me."

Mira: How?

Ivan's Higher Self: Just following my inner voice.

Mira: What is Angel Damian here to assist you with?

Ivan's Higher Self: Protecting from negative energy.

Mira: Please ask him if you have any other angels who work with you and ask them to introduce themselves.

Ivan's Higher Self: There is Angel Michael . . . and . . . that's it.

Mira: What purpose does Angel Michael serve? How does he assist you?

Ivan's Higher Self: He is the one who opens up his wings and just covers me with love. It fills up my heart and my body with love.

Mira: I now want to ask Angel Damian and Angel Michael for any messages that they would like to give Ivan.

Ivan's Higher Self: "Know that we are always there with you. You don't have to worry about not making it, because you are going to make it in every situation. It is always going to go the way it is supposed to go. . . ." That's it. They turned around and now they are walking away.

I love this story. It exemplifies so well that the Higher Self is only the conduit through which the love, light, and healing of All That Is comes to us. When addressing Ivan's questions, I was seemingly conversing only with his Higher Self. Yet the moment I spoke to his angels, they stepped out of the common energy and identified themselves. Their energetic presence was noticeably different, as Ivan's delivery and tone of voice changed as they spoke through him. Ivan's guardian angels had been there the entire time I had been speaking with the Higher Self, supporting the process as part of the whole.

Spirit, on all of its levels of consciousness, is always there to guide and support us, not only during regressions but in every moment of life as well. Often we become so focused on the external world and the input of our thinking mind that we forget how supported we are. As often as possible, remind yourself that you are cradled with love and light. Know it, trust it, and live from that place.

Lisa's Story

Lisa was introduced to the vibration of her Higher Self in a way that was playful and gentle, but memorable for both of us.

At the beginning of our first session, I guided Lisa into a state of relaxation. Once she was focused within, I asked her to describe what she saw in her mind's eye. She saw herself as a little girl who had on a warm wool sweater but bare legs and feet. She didn't like wearing shoes much. She was in the attic hiding, but no one was looking for her. She went a couple of floors down and saw the couple that owned the house and their six children eating dinner. They didn't know she was there. The house she was in was the manor of the estate. Her family was the help. Her mother—a large and soft woman whose clothes always smelled like bread—was the cook at the manor. The little girl felt really loved.

As Lisa was describing to me how loving her mom was, she began to feel a spinning feeling. She said, "I feel like someone picked me up and is spinning me around. It was fun at first but now I feel like I'm going to throw up." It is always my goal that clients are safe and comfortable during their regressions, so I gave Lisa instructions to relax her body and allow for the spinning feeling to dissipate. After a few minutes, Lisa said that her dad was spinning her and that he had finally put her down.

Her dad was big and safe and worked the land. Her cousins, aunts, and uncles lived there, too. Following the abolition of slavery, her ancestors had stayed there on the land in rural Alabama because they had nowhere else to go. Her parents worked hard, and she wanted to help but didn't know what to do. She was not allowed in the kitchen, nor was she allowed to help her dad with farming. The little girl liked to rub her dad's feet at night. With great affection in her voice, she said that he was ticklish. By rubbing his feet, she felt useful and was able to show him how much she loved him.

Lisa was sad to leave her parents when the time came for her to go to college. She went on to become a lawyer who worked on civil rights cases. Even though she was reluctant, she took a job at a law firm in Birmingham, Alabama, representing black families, people no one else would represent and who were not able to pay her much. She said, "I don't like it, but I'm going to do it. It is really important because I'm black and I'm a woman, and I'm really good at my job. There are many people who don't want me to do well. I don't love it, but I know it is important so I'll keep doing it."

She married a man named Charlie who was working on a big civil rights case. They decided not to have children because their work was so important. One day, as they were walking down the street, a man approached them, pulled out a gun, and shot Charlie in the chest. Charlie and Lisa were holding hands—as he went down, Charlie pulled her with him and she fell on top of him. She stayed there until the ambulance came. She was crying, kissing him, and calling his name. Following his death, Lisa continued working on Charlie's cases. It allowed her to feel close to him but also reminded her how much she missed him.

Her parents were long dead and she hadn't stayed in touch with her cousins. She had no one and regretted not having had children. She lived well into her 90s. The morning of her death she was making herself a fried egg for breakfast when she had a heart attack. Her spirit easily slipped out of her body and sat on a chair in the kitchen, waiting to see how long it would be before someone found her body.

Some time passed before a little girl—a neighbor whom Lisa would read to—came to visit and found her dead. Lisa's spirit felt bad for the little girl and attempted to calm her down by sending love to the girl's heart and mentally telling her that all was well. The little girl got the message.

The lesson Lisa's Oversoul learned in that life was that work is very important, but it should never be more important than family. Having people to love and share your life with is paramount.

After the session, Lisa told me that the spinning feeling she'd gotten at the start of the regression had returned shortly after her dad had put her down. Not only that, but it had stayed with her for the rest of the session! I wished she had told me, as I could have given her instructions to center the energy.

As with all clients, I sent Lisa a recording of our session. She e-mailed me back soon after and told me there was a problem with the recording. Twenty-seven minutes into the session, Lisa had said, "There is something . . ." From there on, the recording repeated the word *something* over and over. Nothing else got recorded! The session was almost four hours long, so we had a 3½-hour recording of "something . . . something . . . something"!

When Lisa heard the recording the first time, she had laughed. She remembered the spinning feeling and had a sense that it had caused the recording to skip. I myself was shocked. I record all my sessions directly on my laptop using a professional microphone. Throughout each session, I keep an eye on the laptop screen to make sure the software metrics are working properly. Upon testing the microphone and the software again, the playback was normal. It made absolutely no sense!

Thirteen days after our initial meeting, Lisa was visiting New York City, and we agreed to meet for another session. This time I was prepared to record with two devices—both my laptop and another recorder. In anticipation of her arrival, I brought the spinning energy into my mind. I asked it not to disturb the electronics, but instead to help provide a beneficial session to Lisa. I was determined to have a good recording for her so that she could listen to it in the future.

Once she was relaxed, the scenes began flowing through her mind once again. This time, Lisa saw herself as a ballerina. She was describing her attire, how the theater looked, and how the director was critiquing her performance. A few short moments into the regression, the spinning feeling returned.

"I'm having that feeling of spinning in my chest again," she said. "It's hard to get my breath." I gave her instructions to relax, but the spinning continued.

"It's not a negative energy," she noted. "It's playful. It's joking with me." I was able to calm the energy, but I had to repeat the process several times because the spinning kept returning. I asked Lisa's Higher Self to explain the spinning to me. This is the answer I received:

Lisa's Higher Self: I'm trying to figure out how to explain it. It's her soul energy. People always talk about what happens to the soul when it leaves the body or what actually happens in a body that makes it alive or not alive. It's the spirit . . . it is actual energy. It's the reawakening of that energy that spins. When you stir it up and it starts to move, it's a physical sensation that there's an actual spirit. It's a piece of the bigger soul of everything. It's the piece that's in this body right now. It's the spinning that's the waking up. It's always awake, but it's getting boosted.

Mira: So is the spinning a feeling that she can evoke within herself so she can feel her soul and feel a stronger connection with her Higher Self? Can she just focus on it anytime she wants?

Lisa's Higher Self: Yes, but not if she's doing seven different things. You have to be focused. Human focus is limited just like the life is limited, so it needs your full concentration or almost full, at least in the beginning. It gets easier. It takes your total concentration. That energy is what disrupted the electromagnetic frequencies of the recording before.

I asked the Higher Self whether Lisa's body was able hold this energy permanently. The answer I received was that human bodies cannot hold the enormous energy of their soul for a limitless amount of time. That is why the soul doesn't ever burn out, but bodies do.

As promised, the recording of our second session together did not contain any disruptions.

How to Connect with Your Own Higher Self

You can connect to your Higher Self at any moment, because your Higher Self is really a part of you. It is available to offer you comfort and guidance in every moment. Asking for help reinforces the feeling of connection, allowing you to feel embraced by love and support. The simplest, most powerful way to instantly connect with your Higher Self is to have a third-person dialogue with yourself, pretending that you *are* your Higher Self. Here is an example:

> *Question:* Mira is concerned about her trip and meeting with her new client. What advice could you give her?

Allow for the words to flow without censoring them.

> *Answer:* Mira is concerned because she believes that when she meets this client he will be looking at her with human eyes. Yes, that will inevitably be there. But this person will experience a greater perception than just what the human eye can see. This meeting is a soul meeting, and much work has been done in the dream state to allow for this coming together. The soul recognition will be instant. She need not worry. She only needs to look into his eyes and allow for the heart energies to synchronize. It has all already been orchestrated, and comfort will quickly set in.

This is a real example. At the time, I was working on a project that required me to fly out to Los Angeles to meet with a client. I had never met him before, and yet the project required us to connect and trust one another. I was anxiously anticipating the meeting. Thankfully, the guidance I received through this exercise soothed the anxiety. Several times before the appointed meeting I checked in with my Higher Self for support. The words I imagined my Higher Self saying were always loving and encouraging. The meeting went well, just as my Higher Self had assured me it would. There was an instant feeling of comfort and trust between us, and ever since then our work has been flowing beautifully.

You can do this exercise in writing, or you can have the conversation in your head as often as you can think of during the day. I do both. There are moments when my instincts guide me to sit down and connect with my Higher Self through writing. Yet many more times during the day I allow these third-person dialogues to unfold in my mind. The beauty of playing this game is that the more often you do it, the easier and the greater the clarity of the directions will be. We are always guided; we just rarely pay attention to it. We have become very good at filtering out the love that Source has for us, focusing instead on our aloneness. In that way, we have hypnotized ourselves into feeling isolated and unsupported.

Exercise: Dialogue with Your Higher Self

I suggest approaching this process as a game that you play. The more playful you can be, the better. There is no right or wrong way to talk to your Higher Self. Just play, experiment, and allow yourself to be silly.

There are two ways to do this process: in your mind and on paper. Do the process in your mind when you are looking for a quick check-in with your Higher Self throughout the day. When you want more detailed guidance, set aside ten minutes of quiet time. Have your journal by your side. Begin by taking a deep breath in and slowly let it out. Set the intention to connect with your Higher Self and receive guidance on the question you are facing. Do the steps listed below by writing down both your question and the answer:

1. Ask a question or think of a situation that you want support with. When asking the question, talk about yourself in the third person.

2. Use your imagination and take the perspective of someone who loves you unconditionally, who has your best interests at heart, and who understands the bigger picture of your soul path. You can imagine this to be your Higher Self, a being of light, an angel, a saint, or any being you know will provide you with love, light, and healing energy. Imagine that you *are* that being.

3. Start giving yourself advice, analysis, or support from the perspective of this being who carries you with the deepest, most profound love.

Playing this game allows your guides, angels, and Higher Self to gracefully insert their wisdom and support into your stream of consciousness. Sometimes the words you imagine will sound familiar; it may seem that it is just you talking. Other times it will feel obvious that these words are coming from beyond your own consciousness. It is your Higher Self or a light being nudging you again and again in the direction of your highest good.

I am repeatedly amazed by how workable and powerful this simple technique can be.

Now let's build on this feeling of being one with our Higher Self. In the next chapter we're going to examine how everything reflects us—because it *is* us.

CHAPTER 5

EVERYTHING REFLECTS YOU

As we discussed in the previous chapter, at a soul level we often choose to incarnate with the same group of souls in lifetime after lifetime. We like to travel and grow by sharing experiences with the people we've been with in other lives. As a result, soul groups usually move on up through the levels of consciousness together. The whole is only as strong as its weakest part.

You may recall that in the first life John and I explored together, he was a banker who committed suicide late in life due to loneliness. After he died, we observed as he ascended to a different plane where his friends and family were waiting for him—his soul group. John discovered that his group was ready to move on to a different level of consciousness, but John himself was not. He needed to integrate the issues caused by loneliness in his life as the banker. Because he was not ready to move on, the soul group was not able to continue forward, either.

The commitment to the development of others exists on a global level as well as on the level of the soul group. Souls often return to Earth to be of service and to raise the consciousness of our planet. This can occur even if our own rebirth cycle on Gaia, on Earth, is complete. Of course, a soul can always continue its development on a different plane of existence once its time on Earth is complete, but many decide to stay behind and be of service.

The reason we progress together is because we are all one, each of us part of All That Is. On every subsequent level of existence, the individualization of consciousness decreases. The unity becomes greater and the fractions fewer as we get closer to the One.

The Universe is structured holographically. Each part of the hologram contains the information for the whole. The word *hologram* comes from the Greek word *holos*, "whole." Author Gregg Braden explains that "a hologram is a pattern that is whole and complete unto itself and, at the same time, it is part of an even greater pattern that is whole and complete unto itself, which at the same time is part of an even greater pattern. This pattern can be nonphysical energy or it can be very physical matter."

Each one of us is a facet of a multidimensional hologram. What this means is that within us we contain everything we perceive to be "out there." But everyone and everything that is "out there" also contains us! Because everything is contained in everything, there is really no "out there." There really is just me. I am in everything, and everything is in me. Every flower, every tree, every cloud, every giggling baby, every person, every situation . . . these are all different ways in which I know myself. The Sufi poet Rumi summarized this very beautifully when he said that each of us is not just a drop in the ocean, but we are also the vast and powerful ocean found in every drop.

My clients often experience a return to Oneness during their regressions. Remembering that a person is one with All That Is creates a profound sense of unconditional love. One after another, clients come out of their deep regression states and say that they feel different, that they feel changed, that they have become a new and better person. Hearing this creates fireworks of fulfillment, joy, and gratitude in me. By making space for others to reconnect with the Divine love that they come from, the love that they are, I connect with my own spirit and live my own purpose.

Being in nature and marveling at the perfection that surrounds us also allows us to reconnect with our essence and to remember that we are in unity with All That Is. The melodic birdsong is there to nourish us and lighten our vibrations. Witnessing the exuberance with which everything grows and how nature effortlessly follows its natural impulses, we are reminded that we too are constantly revealing to ourselves more of who we are. We know our own value and goodness beyond any doubt because it permeates every cell of our being. Through the world around us, we can know deeply that we are one with the Universe.

Choose Love Over Judgment

The feeling of being in harmony with our surroundings is harder to sustain when we are among people, living our everyday lives. As the magic dust of a nice walk in nature wears off, we find ourselves right back in that all-too-familiar state of feeling separate, frustrated, anxious, different, and alone. Our minds are quick to analyze, group, and label everything that comes at us. We compare ourselves not only to the people and events we encounter, but also against our mental files—the "shoulds," "coulds," and "woulds." Although the comparison game puts us outside of the stream of well-being, it also serves a very constructive purpose. By comparing things, we get to know our own preferences. These new preferences create new desires in us, and the new desires fuel us with excitement. They propel us into creating our lives and our realities. There will always be contrasts in the world. What's important to know is how to maintain our connection with Source and not be swayed by negative emotions and judgments.

When we judge an event or a person, we really are judging ourselves. Because of our holographic nature, any judgment is self-judgment. We would be unable to perceive what troubles us in others if we did not contain the vibrational equivalent of their energy within us. The judgment we project outward acts upon us inwardly. It is natural to feel dislike when we encounter a person or an event that doesn't match our preferences. Yet knowing our preference on an issue does not mean we have to label it "wrong."

I encourage you to shift your focus from what is troubling on the outside to examining what is the challenge inside you. That person or event is simply a gift from your Higher Self—an effort to make you integrate the opposing beliefs about how your reality should be and align your thoughts and emotions with the true essence of your soul. By taking on this approach to judgment, you allow yourself to stay grounded in the essence of unconditional love. By detaching from swirling negativity, you stay at peace. You can look at others—and yourself—with a very deep and profound understanding. It allows you to reclaim your ability to choose whether to spiral into negative thoughts or to be uplifted by the possibility of knowing yourself in a greater, more joyful way.

Negativity is not a given. We have the right and the ability to choose how we respond to circumstances. Remember, there are no habits, only choices. The moment you become aware of something within you that you're not pleased with, it is no longer hidden. You are conscious of it, and because of that you are able to choose better. It is as simple as that.

With that understanding in our hearts, it is only natural to choose love. For we *are* love. Everything is created out of the life-giving vibration of unconditional love. That is why the best way to express who we are and serve All That Is is to infuse any distressing situation with love. We do this by making the choice to stay in love and to project thoughts of love to those involved. To stay in love, affirm: *I am the warm, welcoming, and allowing energy of love.* By doing this, you help clear the dense energy surrounding any negative occurrence and help raise the consciousness of the whole. You also make it easier for everyone else to follow the same road, because the energetic blueprint already exists.

Putting yourself in this state of mind creates a very profound sense of compassion and connectedness. You will intuitively know that each one of us is doing the best we can in every situation. By staying in the essence of love, we hold the light for everyone else, showing them positive ways to create and experience their realities. If you feel compelled to act and bring changes in the world, act from that wiser, higher ground that exists in you. When you act from a place of love and integrity, your positive energy will attract like-minded visionaries. Together the changes you work toward will make the world a better place.

September 11, 2001

I was at home on the morning of September 11, 2001. It was a warm and sunny day with no sign of what was to come. At that time, I lived a few blocks away from the World Trade Center and could see the Twin Towers from my window. I was physically shaken by the impact and mentally shocked when the planes crashed into the buildings. Later, I watched from my window in horror as the Twin Towers collapsed to the ground in a deafening rumble. An ominous cloud of gray dust filled the air, and suddenly all was invisible.

It was as if time stood still. My reality transformed into a moment of eternal emptiness. The sight of the gray dust covering everything, the difficulty breathing, the sense of confusion, the fear and the instinct to survive, the sounds of the sirens, and the surreal images of rivers of people rushing away to safety—all of these scenes continue to replay in my mind to this day.

The hours and days that followed were difficult. I was not allowed to return to my apartment for three weeks, and the only things I had were the clothes on my back. Yet I have never felt more protected or taken care of in my life. The outpouring of love and support I received was overwhelming.

We all grew up so much because of the events that day. We learned that as human beings, we have the ability to create and destroy—but we also have the ability to overcome any challenge. We learned the important lessons of selflessness, compassion, faith, and above all, love. The cascade of political and cultural changes that followed 9/11 continue to present us with opportunities to learn that there is no division between "us" and "them," and that we are all just people looking for fulfillment.

On the night of September 11, I fell asleep on the floor of a gymnasium thanking God. It is with gratitude in my heart that I remember that day. I am grateful to the brave souls who sacrificed themselves for us to expand our understanding of love, compassion, and power. I am grateful to the people who opened their hearts and found millions of ways to be of service to their brothers and sisters in the days that followed. I am grateful to our Source for nurturing us and giving us the strength to continue in light and love. I hold no fear or hatred because of these events. I extend love and compassion to all. I choose to be the light that uplifts, rather than drown in the mire of fear and negativity.

Finding the Opportunity in Difficult Situations

It is important to bring nonjudgment and acceptance to our everyday interactions, be they with sweethearts, children, co-workers, or the random strangers we pass by. Yet think of all the little ways we criticize and pass judgment, if only in our mind. We judge how people dress, how they wear their hair, what they say, how they earn and spend their money—the list goes on and on. But how dull this world would be if everything were done according to what *you* believe is right! There would be no diversity. Everyone would be a clone of you, and the situation would be terribly monotonous. It wouldn't even be worth interacting with the world because everything would be the same as you.

By validating the diversity we see in others, we can know unity. The beauty of Oneness is in its many-ness. Similar to a puzzle, each one of us fits perfectly into the greater whole. By being true to ourselves—and interacting with the world in that way—we support All That Is. When we do this, it becomes easier to allow others to be who they truly are, too. When I find myself being judgmental of another, all I say is, "How interesting." That person is simply reflecting that there are other possibilities I could choose from. I silently thank the person for yet another way I have witnessed All That Is. Then I graciously move on, focusing on thoughts that excite me and creating the life I choose to live.

There will always be events in our personal lives that put us on edge. Our parents divorcing or selling the family house; our sibling marrying someone we don't approve of; our best friend getting plastic surgery we don't think is necessary; or worse, a loved one developing a debilitating disease. Events like these tend to push us into extreme feelings, creating sleepless nights of worry that isolate us from the experience of well-being and Oneness. When met with challenges like these, I invite you to remember that they are there for a reason. Acknowledge yourself as the masterful co-creator of your circumstances, and take ownership of the situation—even if it's not yet clear why such events are transpiring or how they're helping you grow.

We attract difficult situations because there is something of value for us to learn; they give us the opportunity to be of service to others. Such situations create anxiety because they mirror unresolved issues we carry inside of us. Because we are all one—because the Universe is a hologram—what we are faced with is ourselves. Experiences come into our lives to serve as a reflection of who we are; they allow us to integrate the challenges that remain unresolved. Therefore, we can use these events as an opportunity to know ourselves better, to understand our beliefs, to assimilate them, and to replace them with new ideas that better support who we want to be.

If we do not address such problem situations at their core—at the level of beliefs that define our lives—we continue to re-create the same occurrences no matter how many times we try to tailor things anew. A common example is romantic relationships. For some of us it feels as if we continue to attract the same type of person over and over, and the relationship issues inevitably turn out to be the same. The only solution many of us see is to find a new partner; maybe it will turn out better this time! But rather than going through another painful breakup, we can recognize that the great love we desire lies within us. The answer is not in finding someone new and shiny. We must work on our beliefs and understand what motivates us at our core. We must resolve our own limitations, heal ourselves, and *then* decide whether we would like to stay in our current relationship. Perhaps the old issues will have been taken care of, or perhaps we'll realize that we are ready for something different, knowing that we are now different ourselves.

When a change occurs in one part of the hologram, it is reflected throughout the entire hologram. All of its individualized parts are affected. Therefore, the moment you change your stance, your thoughts, and your beliefs, that change will be mirrored in the situation itself. It will seem as if things have miraculously changed. In truth, the only thing that has changed is you. When we find ourselves in places that are not to our liking, the answer is not to change everyone else—to preach our version of what is right or to attempt to repair what seems broken. Instead, we must acknowledge that the situation mirrors something about us and go within. There we can clean out the cobwebs and shine light into the dusty corners of our stories. We can study our beliefs and intentionally transform them into what we would rather be living. The sooner we do this, the faster the situation will shift.

Exercise: How to Uncover Your Limiting Beliefs and Transform Them

It is critical to know our beliefs because they are the stones with which we build our path in life. They are the foundation on which we construct every experience, thus determining the direction of the small events as well as the entirety of the ultimate masterpiece: this life. Beliefs are nothing more than thoughts, but we assume them to be absolute truths. Some of them are positive and supportive, such as *My mother loves me* or *I am abundantly supported by Source in all that I need.* Other beliefs are counterproductive, acting as invisible walls that confine us.

For this exercise in transforming your beliefs, set aside some quiet time when you will be able to dive within. Plan for a minimum of 30 minutes. The more time you give yourself, the better. Do whatever rituals will affirm your commitment to change and announce to Source that you're present and ready to know yourself, such as lighting a candle or playing soft music. Sit comfortably and have your journal close by. Center yourself by taking a deep breath in, holding it for a moment, and then slowly letting it out.

Think of the challenges you are looking to resolve. Say to yourself, "I am going within to explore all aspects of my limiting beliefs on this subject. I recognize that they are only assumptions." To uncover your limiting beliefs on the subject, ask yourself, "What are my thoughts on this issue? What do I believe is true about this situation? What do I believe is true so that I feel this way?" Then, list your thoughts on the subject on a sheet of paper. Write for as long as you can until you feel that you have said it all.

You've done well, so take a deep breath. Feel how you release the attachment to these ideas as you exhale. Next, direct yourself by saying, "My consciousness is shifting now. I am able to see the ideas, thoughts, and patterns that limit me." Through this expanded perspective, now go back to what you have written and read it slowly. Consciously sift through the words to discover the beliefs that no longer serve you. Either underline them or write them down on a separate piece of paper.

Next, take a few deep breaths and with intent, love, and gratitude for the wisdom that will be given to you, invite your Higher Self to join the process. Freely use your imagination with this part of the process; make up as much stuff as you want. Don't expect for the clouds to part with a lightning bolt and for the voice of God to speak. It might happen, but it isn't necessary. All the answers already exist within you.

Imagine how your Higher Self would communicate with you. Would it put you in its lap? Would it put its hand in yours, or its arm over your shoulder? What is its tone of voice? How does it look? How is it dressed?

Imagine your Higher Self is advising you on which new beliefs to adopt and which old beliefs to part with. Write those ideas down. What would your Higher Self want for you? After you write down these new ways of being, read them out loud to yourself. There is great power in hearing these statements being spoken in your own voice. To complete the process, say to yourself with conviction and trust, "It is with ease that I transform my beliefs. I am the person who has these new thoughts and beliefs. My life is the product of these new beliefs, and everywhere I turn I see the results these thoughts have created."

Finally, trust this shift within yourself. Remember, trust is the gate that directs the flow of your God-given ability to create your life. What you trust in is what you create. Reinforce your trust by intentionally repeating those new thoughts to yourself. When you think these thoughts, you will feel good. You will feel optimistic and expanded. These joyous feelings are a confirmation that when you allow the energy of the chosen thought to flow through you, you are in vibrational alignment with your Higher Self, with your true essence.

Most important, act on your new beliefs. Act as if you are a person who has always had these beliefs. Act as the person who is already living the life that you prefer.

By saying to yourself that it is easy for you to change your beliefs, you're putting in place the *ultimate* belief: the belief that you are in charge of your reality. That you are the one who chooses. When transforming your beliefs, you don't need to go through a complicated process beyond these few simple steps. If you believe that transformation needs to be a long and rigorous process, you will certainly experience it that way. But I am here to assure you that it doesn't have to be. The moment you have seen things through a new perspective, your consciousness has expanded. Why go back? You have stepped into a new parallel reality and have literally become a new person. Trust that and act like it. The only permission you need to change is your own. Know that you *are* your new beliefs, and start making choices from that place of knowing. And remember: the Universe is a hologram. The moment you decide that you have changed, everything around you will happily confirm that for you.

Judy's Story

Sometimes we witness circumstances that bring up anxiety and fear in those around us. It's helpful to assume that we've attracted these situations in order to be of service. It is a socially acceptable response to offer sympathy to others or to feel guilty for having more than they do. Yet such offerings only reinforce the negativity of the situation. Instead, we can remain grounded in our connection with the Infinite. Doing so puts us in the best possible position to be of assistance.

We need not look to save anyone, or to feel responsible. Nor do we need to feel guilty that we're better attuned to abundance and support. Instead, we can find the possibility of being truly compassionate. Being compassionate means being able to see beauty, greatness, and potential where everyone else sees lack and limitations. We can see behind the masks of failure, sickness, and not-enough-ness to the true strength underneath. All of our choices—yes, even the choice to experience disease and disharmony—are made from a position of strength because we are eternal. Nothing could ever break or eradicate us. Knowing this, we can trust that no matter how suffocating the situation, it is serving those involved.

On a soul level, each of us is deeply aware of our own strength. We know that challenges are but opportunities for growth. The level to which we allow ourselves to be immersed in negativity is proportionate to the level at which we can experience illumination, ascension, and expansion. Judy's story is an example of this profound truth.

Judy was a young woman with an impressive—and stressful—career in law enforcement when she was diagnosed with a brain aneurysm. A blood vessel in her brain had expanded dramatically and its walls had become very thin. When the doctor gave her the news, Judy didn't know whether to cry, worry, or simply accept that her next breath could be her last. Within a couple of weeks—which felt like an eternity to her and her family—she had an operation performed by the best neurosurgeon in the country. The operation was a success in that the aneurysm was removed. But in a rare twist, she had a stroke during the surgery. When she awoke from the procedure, Judy was completely paralyzed. Now, several years later, the paralysis only lingers on the left side of her body. Through persistence and the power of her spirit, she became able to walk. Yet she still wears a brace on her left leg, and she continues to have limited mobility in her left arm.

During our session together, Judy saw herself as a young woman who lived on a farm outside of a small town in Montana in the 1800s. She described in great detail the simple life she lived—her children, her husband, the garden, the nearby town, and how everything was dry and covered with dust. I asked her Higher Self why she accessed this lifetime as opposed to any other. The answer was simple yet very important for Judy: Her Higher Self told her that it wanted to show her how strong she is. It told her that she had chosen to experience her present physical challenges so that she could grow spiritually. Her aneurysm and her stroke were not caused by past karma, nor were they the result of God punishing her for her sins. They were the confident creation of a star seeking to shine even brighter. Her Higher Self told her that she is very strong emotionally, mentally, and physically. It assured her that everything was just right, and that she was loved unconditionally.

Because of her medical history and her dedication to living from her spirit, Judy has grown so much that her Higher Self has encouraged her to inspire and uplift others. Needless to say, Judy's session was deeply healing for her. I myself felt honored to have witnessed such a brave and beautiful soul.

We Are All Vibrations

When we are loving and compassionate, we know that in the big scheme of things everyone and everything is right and perfect. Our vibration becomes the vibration of Oneness and unconditional love. By immersing in the stream of well-being and connectedness, we affect not only those around us but also the entirety of All That Is.

Even without words, we are constantly communicating with one another. In fact, the majority of the information we exchange is through our energy field: A study conducted at UCLA showed that 93 percent of our communication is based on nonverbal exchanges. Of course, this makes sense. When we are in the presence of someone warm and kind, we feel welcomed. In a few short moments we become uplifted, as our energy begins to match theirs. When, on the other hand, we are in the presence of someone who is critical, cynical, and negative, we feel as if we have been sucked into his or her dense vibration. All we want to do is run away! A positive attitude unifies and raises others' energy levels. We become better versions of ourselves, simply by being in the presence of positivity.

There are constructive, supportive, and fulfilling ways to be in any situation. When we model those ways for others, we help them realize that they prefer to operate on a higher resonance level as well. From there, they can consciously use their power to create circumstances that support them.

As you may already know, change must come from within. No change in one's personality or life can be imposed from the outside. Nagging hardly ever works as a strategy to convey possibilities for change—or to maintain a good relationship. It may bring the desired result, but at a heavy price because it can be damaging to the other person's sense of self. But by connecting with another from a place of love and compassion, you can encourage genuine transformation. It doesn't matter whether that person is ready to make the leap; as long as you stay grounded in your loving essence, without judging or forcing, you will bring grace and ease. There is no hurry. After all, we have an eternity to get where we're going.

○

Because we are all one, we are always immersed in the stream of knowingness, a shared field of consciousness that connects us all. This web of information is constantly being created and experienced by all individualized expressions of the consciousness of God, of All. As one with this whole, you too can choose to be supported and nourished by this vastness.

During a series of experiments that resulted in one of the most important discoveries of the 20th century, physicist Alain Aspect set out to scientifically prove something we have intuitively understood for centuries. In 1982, Aspect's experiment demonstrated Bell's theorem of inequality, showing that under certain conditions particles are able to instantaneously "communicate" with each other regardless of the distance separating them, completely unconcerned with any notion of space and time! This meant that the long-accepted physics principle of locality—which states that an object is influenced directly only by its immediate surroundings—no longer held true. Aspect's discovery lent support to the theories known as quantum nonlocality and quantum entanglement.

Furthermore, these experiments shattered the validity of Albert Einstein's theory of special relativity, which asserts that no material or energy can travel faster than the speed of light. They showed not that energy *could* travel that fast; instead, they proved that speed and time as limiting factors are *irrelevant*. Objects are instantaneously connected, regardless of the space and time between them.

"How do these particles communicate?" everyone asked. The question set the scientific community abuzz. David Bohm, another physicist, offered an explanation. Particles respond to each other in this way not because they are somehow mysteriously sending each other signals, but because they are extensions of the same one thing. According to him, at a deeper level all seemingly separate objects are interconnected. At a fundamental level, human beings and whales and trees and fireflies are all vibrations in the same quantum field—a vast, inexhaustible reservoir of energy. As vibrations, we constantly communicate with this field and all its living and nonliving representations. The field connects everything with everything else, like a vast web. At the same time, everything originates from the field and is fueled by the interactions between particles in the field. It's easy to see why, when scientists speak about the field, they might describe it as God—the One, knowing itself as All That Is.

Allowing for Our Intuitive Nature

You and I are connected to this same vast web. As such, we are infinitely intuitive. Yes—*you are intuitive!* Being psychic is not something extraordinary; it's not something weird that happens to only a few people. We are all intuitive, whether we know it or not. It is already part of our blueprint. It is our nature and our heritage.

We have been very successful in straitjacketing this natural connection, blocking it with all kinds of limiting beliefs, fears, and stories. However, if you're interested in allowing for a greater intuitive awareness, there are steps you can take. First, explore other lives where you may have been hurt or shut down for knowing the unseen. I can think of several clients who saw themselves persecuted for their psychic abilities in past lives. After releasing the fears of standing out and speaking up, they've stepped into their true intuitive potential and have let the Divine back in.

I personally experienced such a regression, which released a tremendous fear of being harmed for being myself. I visited a lifetime where, as a white woman, I was studying healing herbs with a medicine woman from a Native American tribe. I was in love with a man from that tribe, and so rejected the advances of a white suitor who wanted to marry me. In his anger and hurt, he exacted revenge by painting me as a witch, and my end quickly came. Clearing that block helped me become comfortable with my intuitive side.

Another story I want to share with you comes from Bianca, a beautiful Italian woman. At the beginning of our session together, she shared with horror how her hair had been falling out. During the regression, my client experienced a life where she and a friend were able to see into the future and help people heal. Rather than being appreciated and treasured by their community, they were burned at the stake. Right before setting them on fire, the executors cut off their hair. At that point in the regression, Bianca was agonizing that by cutting off her hair they were taking away her powers. The final moments of that life were gruesome, and the session was a very emotional experience for Bianca. The Higher Self later explained that human hair is a physical representation of the antennas through which we connect with All That Is.

Before our session, Bianca had told me that she was aware of her ability to heal people, yet something was stopping her. After witnessing this life, she realized she'd been subconsciously terrified that she would be killed again. The hair loss was a way of protecting herself, because it cut off her ability to connect to the Divine. We worked on releasing these beliefs and guiding her to find safety in her connection with God.

Thus, the first step in developing our intuitive powers is to release any fears that have accumulated due to past soul experiences. The second step is to identify and release any fears and negative beliefs we currently have about our psychic abilities. Start by repeating the exercise found earlier in this chapter (on page 84). This exercise allowed me to release emotional stories from my childhood, along with the beliefs that have held me back from trusting the Divine to freely move through me. Combining past-life and present-incarnation clearings will powerfully and effectively release any need to seek safety in separation.

Every molecule in your body is connected to all of existence. You originate from the same energy field as all creation, and thus you are forever inseparably connected with it all. As a result, you know everything and you feel everything. Affirm for yourself that you are connected and that you have within you a knowing that can assist and guide you. Trust your instincts. Be spontaneous: play with it, nurture it, enjoy it, and be amused by it. In doing so, you freely give expression to your knowingness, to the energy field of All That Is. You give it permission to move through you and find form in ways that serve you. We are all part of the same ever-expanding, ever-changing field of consciousness. You are one with All That Is, and All That Is knows you as a valuable, treasured, and beloved part of It. Because of that, All That Is seeks to serve you and support you in becoming who you are meant to be.

The Oneness of You

While learning to merge your Oneness with All That Is, I invite you to also focus on the Oneness of *you*. You are the beautiful dance of mind, body, and spirit. Your mind is logical. It serves you in very practical ways, allowing you to navigate through the physicality of your existence. Your body is the vehicle through which the Divine gets to play in the world, to mold and experience the material. And your spirit breathes life, purpose, love, and guidance into the unfolding of the three. While they may seem separate, all three of these aspects are part of the Oneness that is *you*.

Some among us march through life under the banner of "more." These insatiable beings are always looking for more power, more recognition, and more belongings. They rely exclusively on the mind—on the ability to achieve through the sheer power of will. Spirit is dismissed; after all, it cannot be known, measured, and analyzed in a corporate boardroom with charts and graphs. God is the greatest mystery, and these types aren't into mystery.

But we spiritual people are no saints, either. Once we discover our glorious essence, we often forget that we exist in a physical world, too. That we have chosen to be here for a purpose. Most of us have abandoned the left-brained life, swinging with unchecked exuberance toward the right-brained state of nirvana. We live from our souls and discount the importance of our minds. But Source created human beings with thinking minds so that Spirit can have an ever-greater opportunity for learning and growth. We must learn to use *all* the gifts we've been given.

And regardless of whether we're head- or soul-oriented, we have most likely hurt, abused, or neglected our bodies at some point on this earthly journey. How different our world would be if we were taught that our bodies were sacred vessels! We would have a different relationship with food, alcohol, drugs, and medicines. We would know our sexuality for its beauty and bliss. Instead, we deny our bodies and take them for granted. We must remember that the body is the vehicle expressing our soul's mission.

Lisa, whom you were introduced to in Chapter 4, was abusing her body and feeling disconnected from it when she came to see me. Conversing with her Higher Self, I inquired about her challenges, and this is what was said about the human body:

> There's this idea that the spirit is grander than the body . . . but in this life, the spirit is only as strong as the body. There's mutual love and need. Being spiritual will only go so far, if the same love and energy can't be cultivated in her body and for her body. She needs to be doing anything that is a positive channeling of energy through the body . . . anything that's a practice

of reconnecting the mind, the body, and the spirit together. The yoga is good. The meditation is good. If it's a run, it should be to notice how it feels to take the air in and out of the lungs and not how many blocks to go. Connect and rejoice in the way the body works, not trying to control it, not trying to demand things of it. These are all things we do when we've disconnected and we're trying to fill up again, and they don't work. They just breed more and more negativity.

If you tend to neglect your own body, here's something for you to try. Many of us like to think of the body as the container that holds the spirit. In reality, the soul holds the body. The soul is the one that creates the body and the mind; the body exists *in* the spirit. Now, think about your body through the eyes of your soul. Just like a parent, the Creator always loves its creations unconditionally. Your spirit loves your body. By contemplating the image of your spirit holding your body in its energy with love, your mind will align with this new way of thinking. Having this image in your mind will allow you to mold your relationship with your body into a more positive one.

You have chosen to be born in an exciting time in human history—you have come to partake in the evolution of Oneness. For centuries we have been forgetting our Oneness with All That Is, and denying the Divine trinity of mind, body, and soul. The transcendence of this separation begins with you. Reach up and reach within. Have a mind open to the help of intuition; be always ready to ask for assistance from the Unseen. Do not leave your spirit sitting on the bookshelf after you're done reading an inspirational book. *Live* your spirit.

Bring your soul with you into every physical activity. Exercise knowing that you're strengthening your body so that it can handle the higher vibrations of consciousness that you're reaching with your soul. Experience lovemaking as an exhilarating representation of merging into Oneness with All That Is. Choose foods alive with consciousness that resonate with the ascension of you. Eat mindfully. Choose water over any other drink because it purifies you and grounds you to commune with Gaia.

Bring harmony in your mind, your body, and your spirit, and bring balance among these three. Create a new deal among the three of them. In a moment of meditation, address each one and propose to it that life would be a lot more joyful and easy if the three were to collaborate and support one another rather than compete for your attention through body aches or ego tantrums. Tell your beautiful mind that it is really valued and its concerns will always be heard, that it is doing an excellent job of protecting you and keeping you safe. Assure it that it is not alone, and that it does not need to carry the burden of figuring out your life all on its own. It has the support of its most faithful and loving ally: your soul. Thank your body for tirelessly being of service to you and for knowing how to heal itself and maintain your well-being. Let your mind promise your body that it will make loving choices. Then have your mind and body assure your spirit that they trust it, that they will let it shine and guide the way.

Who is conducting the negotiations, you ask? Your soul. It is your soul that sees the bigger picture and creates life through the other two. By creating this new contract among the three sacred parts of you, you will raise yourself into Oneness.

Albert's Story

Albert came to see me with a very specific goal in mind: he wanted to understand the reason why he had prostate cancer. The previous seven years had been a tale of radiation treatments, countless tests, bad news, and, worst of all, fear—great fear. His session was profound and transformative. Albert received information about the energetic and emotional misalignments that caused the cancer and experienced a very powerful emotional healing. That in itself would have been enough to call the session a success, but something else made his experience even more remarkable.

During the session, Albert experienced what it feels like to be one with Source. His regression began with him perceiving himself as a man who was in a bright chamber inside a pyramid:

It feels like a religious, sacred place. I am humbled. There is a pedestal in the middle of the room going up, made of white stone. The pedestal looks like a rectangular column. It is very big. It is the core of this building, and it is going up into the roof. It seems like the roof opens to the sky. There is energy in the room. The energy feels warm, like sunlight on a summer day.

I am at the top of the rectangular column now . . . I am walking to the middle of the platform. I am looking up toward what I'm guessing is the apex of the pyramid. I am holding my arms up. It feels . . . this expansion of me. I have my arms up and out and my legs are spread. I am buzzing with energy. I feel good. I feel like I somehow want to expand.

My mind is out in space now. It took me out in space but I don't think it took my body out there. I am in the darkness of space now. I see stars. It's unbelievable! I feel this tremendous energy. I'm feeling this connection, this awesome connection. I am in the middle of everything. I am connected to everything and it's amazing! It feels vast. It feels inexplicably right to be here.

The connection is a powerful emotional feeling. It also feels logical at the same time. It is wonderful and emotionally overwhelming in a positive way, and it is logically comforting because it feels right. I feel like I want to expand out into everything and at the same time I want to suck everything into me. It is wonderful! It's like being an integral part of the Universe but not a thing in it . . . the Universe feels like a part of me. I feel like I can wiggle my fingers and I would see the stars jiggle around me. Everything is totally connected.

Albert could feel his "individual self" as well as the bigger energy of All That Is. But soon he wanted to expand out into the Oneness more, and he discovered that he was afraid. As much as he wanted to feel the energy all around him, he also didn't want to lose his identity. Still, he pushed forward:

There's a brightness that is almost blinding. It is white, bright . . . like a milky-white brightness. It is around me. It is bright, crisp, clean, and pure. Wow! It is so bright, it is unbelievable! Oh, my God! Oh, jeez . . . ! Oh, my God! Oh . . . ! Oh, my God! Oh!

I am a part of an energy that is unbelievable. It is milky-white brightness. It is vibrating in a very subtle way but very powerfully. I can't contain myself anymore. I am intermixed with this. It is bigger than me. It is clean—so clean, so pure! There is nothing else. It is just this whiteness. I can almost perceive myself in it but not like before. I am a vague outline of that body, but it is barely there. The vibration is almost too much to handle. The vibration is a little uncomfortable, but the feeling is wonderful. It is bliss. It is contradictory, but it is bliss in a boring way because nothing is happening. It is exciting, wonderful nothingness. The feeling of being in this light is beautiful because it is so clean. There is nothing impure . . . there is nothing! I don't see anything! There is nothing to mar it. It is perfect and it's clean. The cleanliness is so reassuring and refreshing. It is so good. There is nothing happening. It feels wonderful.

I am slightly outside of it now. I am still with it, but now I can feel a little more distinctness of myself. Earlier I kept on thinking this energy is God, but I thought it is my mind deducing that. Now I do feel it is God. And I am before God in a way. That's why I've come out of it a little bit. In order to perceive it as God, I had to come out of it. I was in it before. I was one with it. I felt no distinction with anything. Now I am a little bit out of it, and I perceive it as this otherness that is so much bigger than me. It feels totally benevolent and loving. I still feel good, but nothing like I did when I was with it. The contrast is unbelievable. Being outside of it is still a wonderful feeling, but it is so pitiful compared to what it feels like inside it.

Albert was having a direct experience of the Oneness of everything. Soon, he told me that he had "detached" somewhat, and suddenly he recognized how lonely it is to be "outside of that"— to be separate. I asked him why, if the Oneness is so wonderful, do we leave it? Albert responded:

When I was in it, I was not aware of it. I had to step out of it to perceive it. I was aware of feeling good, but it felt like nothingness. It was beautiful, but it was one state of being. It was a beautiful state of being, but it was nondimensional. A perfect blandness . . . when I step out of it, the lack of it impressed upon me the beauty of it. I had to know what it feels like to be one with that energy and then to know what it feels like not to have it, in order to truly understand and appreciate what it is. Because in and of itself, from within it there is nothing. When you step out of it, you begin to comprehend the awesomeness of it and the perfection of it, and the goodness of it.

Oh, God! From out here it is not bland at all! From outside it is beautiful. It was beautiful inside, but it was different. I couldn't perceive it from within. I could feel it, and I could feel it was good. I could not perceive it because it is All That Is, and it is nothing but bright white light and a vibration. When I step out of it I want to be back in it, but I have a better sense of what it is when I am outside of it than when I am in it. I guess that makes sense. When you are in a building you cannot have an understanding of the building you're in until you step outside of it. That is the image I am getting right now. When you're in the Light you don't know it. You don't know what it is. You step out of it and you are awestruck. And then you want to go back.

After the Oneness experience was complete, I suggested that Albert merge his energy with the energy of his Higher Self and the highest level of love, wisdom, and healing available to him. Once that connection was established, I asked about the prostate cancer. I was told that this present life was the one and only incarnation Albert's soul was to have on Earth, that he had come here to energetically assist humankind in the expansion of consciousness. But now that it was limited to the confines of a human body, Albert's spirit greatly missed the feeling of Oneness.

As a young man he had discovered that drinking simulated the breaking of that physical boundary, bringing a brief experience of elation. Unconsciously, he assumed that the more he drank, the greater the expansion of his spirit would be. Around that same time, he discovered that sex provided a similar feeling of expansion. Soon, both sex and drinking became obsessions for him. Although he'd given up alcohol years before, the sex obsession had continued into his marriage. Ashamed of this part of himself, he made a subconscious effort to kill his mojo. He developed erectile dysfunction and, later, prostate cancer.

During Albert's session, however, the layers of emotional and mental trauma caused by the sexual repression were removed—from his body, his energy field, and his consciousness. Albert was advised by his Higher Self to make it a daily practice to connect to the feeling of interconnectedness he experienced during the regression. There, his Higher Self explained, he would find the true sustenance he needed.

Exercise: Meditation for Oneness

The idea that everything is energy and that everything is interconnected may be familiar to you. You may even believe in it. But have you ever experienced it? There is a significant difference between understanding something intellectually and having the deep, visceral knowledge that comes from direct experience. If having this experience intrigues you, I suggest the following meditation for connecting with All That Is.

Set aside 20 minutes of quiet time. Sit or lie down comfortably. Have your journal nearby to write down your experience or any insights or visions. Set the intention that you will explore freely, knowing that you are safe. Begin by relaxing your body. Take a few slow breaths in. Remind yourself that you know the way within. Use your imagination freely and add as many details as you desire.

Close your eyes and imagine the brightly lit chamber inside a pyramid that Albert described in his regression. Imagine the rectangular pedestal going up in the air. Tell yourself that this is a portal that will allow you to transcend time and space. State your intention to connect with the All through this experience. Find the stairs that lead to the top of the pedestal, and climb them with ease. When you reach the top, gaze up and see what is above you. Walk to the center, spread your legs in a powerful stance, and spread your arms up and out. Allow your consciousness to expand and reach up and up.

If the images and feelings begin to flow in your mind, enjoy them. Without striving for a particular result, let them evolve and infuse you with their magic. If you're uncertain as to what you are supposed to see and experience, allow your imagination to guide you. Ask yourself what Oneness would feel like. Let yourself paint as many details as you can. Do not dismiss the process just because you are imagining it. Because of the simultaneity of time, everything imaginable already exists. Imagination is a playful way to connect to what already exists, and to bring it into your reality. Stay with the joyful creation of the images in your mind. Before you know it, you will be deeply feeling the interrelatedness of All.

When you feel ready to come back to waking consciousness, allow yourself to slowly orient to the present moment. Become aware of your body and your surroundings. If you feel moved, describe your experience in your journal.

Connecting to All That Is will feed your spirit with the feeling of being unconditionally loved, supported, and part of the All. Once you have this experience, you will know for yourself what Albert meant when he said, "Everything is totally connected."

In this chapter we explored the different aspects of the notion of Oneness—the principle that everything reflects you. We examined the concept of Oneness through holograms and quantum physics, and saw that diversity creates Oneness. We dove into ways to maintain a sense of peace when faced with people and situations that provoke negative responses in us. This led us into a discussion on how to reveal our limiting beliefs and transform them. Now let's continue our explorations of consciousness and see what part forgiveness plays in our ability to merge into Oneness.

○○○

CHAPTER 6

FORGIVE YOURSELF AND OTHERS

My beautiful sister, Ellie, whom I absolutely adore, lives in Chicago and is a member of a charitable organization that does excellent philanthropic work. I wanted to support their activities, so I donated a regression session to one of their auctions. After the auction Ellie told me that the session had generated excitement and I should be hearing from the winner directly. I knew that, whoever it was, the winner would reach out to me exactly when the time was right.

Months passed. Ellie was pregnant with her second child and her due date was approaching, so I went to Chicago to be with my family and share in the joy of my niece's birth. On the day I arrived, I received an e-mail from Lisa (whom I talked about earlier in the book). She said that she was the one who had won the auction, and that she was ready to schedule her session. What perfect timing! I was there in Chicago, with a relatively free schedule, so we could meet in person.

Lisa was a beautiful woman in her early 30s, with blonde hair and blue eyes. She represented the perfect balance of a bright intellect and a spiritual openness. She had grown up in the Midwest and had attended one of the most prestigious universities in the U.S. She began her career in marketing but had found little satisfaction in it, so she became a teacher instead.

In her teenage years—as she began taking on a more womanly shape—Lisa began feeling very uncomfortable in her body. She compared it to having a pair of wet jeans on that you just want to take off. When she was 16, Lisa's family went out to dinner at a fondue restaurant. Everyone overate that night, and when they got home they made themselves throw up in order to feel better. That night Lisa learned how she could have control over the body she hated so much, and so began her incredibly troubled relationship with food.

For 15 years, mealtimes had been moments of great anxiety for Lisa. She had been in therapy and tried many different ways to resolve the issue, but except for a brief period of time she had never really felt healthy and whole. Lisa and her husband had tried to start a family, but she had had several miscarriages. Hearing that, I wasn't surprised; how could a body that was so hated create something so desired? Lisa's body issues were like an ominous shadow she couldn't get away from. I knew that the answers—and the healing—could be provided through our session. I advised her to approach the regression with trust and openness.

In our session, Lisa connected with several counterparts. Earlier in the book I described her life as the civil rights lawyer, where she learned how important it was to have family and friends to love and share with. But she saw another powerful life as well: that of an unhappy male banker at the turn of the 20th century. It served as a cautionary tale about what the lack of forgiveness can do.

The banker lived in London. He had everything he could have wanted—money, a family, a prestigious job—but he was filled with anger. Watching his life leading up to his death in the 1930s, Lisa reported on how his body was deteriorating—rotting from the inside out—due to all the anger he was carrying. He was not able to forgive others. He was not able to forgive himself. He simply held on to the negativity. The obvious danger of this negative mind-set is the deterioration of the body and the creation of diseases. As the banker said, "It's hard to breathe because it's just hollow. [The anger] sat there so long that it's just cleaned everything out. It hurts my organs on the inside, too. It's a very physical destruction. Everything seems shriveled on the inside."

I believe that Lisa connected with this life to become aware of what her own hatred toward her body could create. But another more subtle—but equally damaging—danger for her was that of removing herself from the closeness of her family because of food issues and beliefs about herself. By not loving herself, she was creating a barrier between her family's love for her and her ability to experience it.

I asked Lisa what she took away from the life of her banker counterpart. She responded, "What definitely sticks is the power, intensity, and poison with which anger can overtake us. Without check, it can grow and grow—especially if there is negative space in someone's consciousness. If there is absence of love and connection and relationships, anger will grow rampant like weeds. I think that as cautious as we have to be with anger, we can be carefree with the love we have. In fact, it's important to share it as much as possible, especially where it is lacking."

Spoken like a true sage! We could all use some meditation on these words and apply their wisdom in our lives. Yet how do we pull the weeds of anger? How do we allow our love to flow ever more freely and powerfully? The answer, I have discovered, is through forgiveness.

The anger, resentment, and blame we carry inside affects us more than the people we're angry with. When we carry hatred, bitterness, and thoughts of revenge, we're hurting *ourselves*. These thoughts and energies weaken us. They create illnesses in our bodies and prevent us from fully being present in the moment, feeling empowered, and creating the lives we want. Forgiveness is the act of letting go of these thoughts we carry around with us. By moving from blame to love, we free ourselves. Sending thoughts of love is the most healing thing we can do. As you will read later in this chapter, forgiving is one of the most important tools of spiritual growth. It clears the way of all that does not belong on the path of ascending into Oneness with Source.

Lisa's regression shows us how important it is to forgive ourselves and others. It also teaches us something else: that it is never too late to forgive.

Working with Our Counterparts

Because time is linear in our perception, we see the lives of our counterparts as complete and finished. But as we've discussed at length, all the lives created by our Oversoul are ongoing, be they in the same year, the same decade, or many centuries apart.

All lives exist simultaneously in the current moment in which you're reading this sentence. Because lives are ongoing, the story of a life is never "complete." Every moment of every life is open to interpretation—it is open to new possibilities, new choices, and new outcomes.

When clients visit with the life of a counterpart and describe it to me, they are only visiting with one of the possible story lines, one of the probabilities of that life. To some this concept may be difficult to grasp. If that's the case, don't spend too much time on it. For now, just know that you have the power to send love, healing thoughts, wisdom, and different perspectives to your counterparts. You and your counterparts share a similar soul frequency, because you are creations of the same Oversoul. Therefore, you have the innate ability to instantaneously connect with them. If you have experienced a traumatic life during a regression, for example, you have seen only one possible outcome of that life. You can communicate to your counterparts that there are other possibilities and other avenues to take. Send them love. Send them light. Send them peace.

During Lisa's regression, I asked the banker how things could have been different in his life. He responded, "I was thinking it could be different if I could just flip a switch or something. I have a sense that that's possible, yet I don't know how to do it." A few days later, I e-mailed Lisa and encouraged her to send feelings of love and hope to her counterpart when she meditates, to be the one who flips the switch for him. Not too long afterward, I heard back from her.

"Your suggestion to send energy—positive, healing energy— to him actually did flip a switch, in *me!*" Lisa reported. Apparently, my remark had reminded her that there is always a potential that could be born in what would seem to be a completed life story. We think of possibilities awaiting to be materialized only when we reflect on the future. But if time is simultaneous and a soul counterpart's life is presently unfolding, then a new choice they make could create a new possible outcome for that lifetime—an outcome that was different from the version of that life Lisa had become aware of.

"I hadn't thought he needed any help," she said. "I was think-ing linearly and thought that his struggles were no longer on-going. It's funny how easy it is to snap back into our 'I'm just me in my body and that's all I have to concern myself with' mode."

Lisa decided to send thoughts of encouragement and support to her banker counterparts. You too can do that at any time. Con-sider doing so while in quiet moments of meditation, or whenever you think of that life. That is exactly what Tala did, as we will discuss next.

Tala's Story

Sometimes the urge to assist a counterpart arises spontaneous-ly. My client Tala hadn't considered the idea of soul counterparts assisting one another, yet the moment her counterpart was in emotional turmoil, her innate wisdom guided her.

Tala was experiencing life as a farmer named Bob, whose be-loved wife was dying. He prayed to God to save her, but she died anyway. Farmer Bob felt bitter and betrayed by God, but he also felt somehow responsible for his wife's death. Upon hearing this,

Tala began speaking directly to her counterpart about letting go, and about love and forgiveness:

> *Tala:* Farmer Bob, you didn't do anything wrong. You loved your wife so much. You didn't do anything wrong. You have to forgive yourself. You've *got* to forgive yourself. Please, for me! For you! Farmer Bob, you can forgive yourself. It was her time. You can live, farmer Bob. She lives in you. Forever. She is always with you. She loves you so much, too. And now you are feeling it. You are feeling it, farmer Bob. I see that you're smiling! It is okay now.

After Tala came out of the trance, I asked her what prompted her to help farmer Bob heal. She simply said, "If he heals, I am healed."

We've all experienced a moment of hope and light in the darkest of days. Who knows? Perhaps such transitions have been prompted by a counterpart who flipped the switch in us—urging us to forgive, supporting us with their love and healing. Be that support for your counterparts. Extend love and kindness toward them. Encourage them to forgive themselves and to forgive everyone else. You never know what new possibilities your energy may create.

The Importance of Forgiving Ourselves

We all know that it's important to forgive those who have wronged us. For most of us it's a challenge to forgive, but once we do we feel lighter and freer. It gives us peace of mind and the ability to move on in our lives, rather than remain a victim of people and circumstances.

The first reason forgiveness is a challenge for people is because we assume it needs to be difficult. This is a cultural belief: "Everyone knows it is hard to forgive, so why would it be different for me?" We elect to hold on to our hurt egos—to the sad stories we tell—because that's what everyone else is doing and we think it's the right thing to do. It does not benefit us in any way, but we continue to do it. The solution is simple: Tell yourself it's easy to forgive. It's a good belief to have, so choose to hold it as your truth. You originate from a place of Oneness, a place where you have no reason to hold yourself separate from anyone else. It's already in your essence to forgive, because there is no need to punish any part of yourself.

The second reason we find it hard to forgive is that we only focus on the first step of the process—forgiving the other. We were never told how important it is to also forgive *ourselves*. Forgiveness is a two-sided coin. No forgiveness is complete when we only focus on forgiving others.

After the life as the banker, Lisa went on to experience the life of a teenager named Kelly. It was the 1950s, and Kelly was a beautiful, "girly" 16-year-old with a boyfriend named Jim. Tragically, her life ended far too soon. Lisa saw Kelly in the back of Jim's car on a night when they had been planning to go to the drive-in. Instead, they had gone to the woods to have sex for the first time. Too late, Kelly decided she didn't want to go through with it—and she began to panic. Jim was trying to calm her down, but she thought he was trying to force himself on her. In his attempt to settle her, he accidentally snapped her neck and killed her.

In a state of panic, Jim contacted Kelly's brother for help. Her brother helped Jim bury Kelly's body and lied to her parents about what had happened. They never found Kelly's remains.

Lisa told me that she saw herself as Kelly, now a disembodied spirit, standing in the family kitchen listening to a conversation between her brother and their parents. She was witnessing with disbelief the lies her brother was weaving about her death—and her parents' apparent acceptance. When she had heard enough, she stormed out of the house.

Yet something interesting happened as she crossed the threshold of the house. In that moment, Kelly's spirit chose to forgive Jim, her brother, and her parents. Lisa experienced an immediate sense of being lighter. Later, when I spoke with Lisa's Higher Self, I asked it to tell me more about what had happened in that moment of forgiveness:

> *Lisa's Higher Self:* On a spiritual level forgiveness is immediate.

> *Mira:* Why is it immediate? What makes it immediate?

Lisa's Higher Self: Because the Spirit has no purpose to punish a part of itself. And we're all part of each other.

When I heard this I was filled with elation. I honestly felt as
if a choir of angels were singing a heavenly tune in my mind! *The
Spirit has no purpose to punish a part of itself because we're all part
of each other.* That is why forgiveness is instant in the afterlife. A
million thoughts rushed through my mind. One was a sense of
gratitude for being offered such a deep and profound understanding. Another was the desire to tell people that it really *is* important
that we stop hurting each other and begin to forgive.

Lisa's Higher Self went on:

Lisa's Higher Self: When you forgive something, it's totally
over. To truly forgive something is a very difficult, human, rational thing to do. You can say you forgive somebody, but it
seems the human tendency is to keep a piece of that in some
way, to teach us something, to be more guarded. "Yeah, I forgive
you, but you'll get yours in the end" kind of thinking. It's a very
human tendency. But when we really forgive, it means it's over.
You forgive him. You've let go of carrying something that you
don't need to carry with you anymore.

It seems like a very simple thing to know, but it's actually
an extraordinarily difficult thing to practice. That may be why
many people pray to be strong enough to actually forgive on
a spiritual level—because that's where it's an easier thing to
do. It's not that you forget that something has ever happened.
You just don't carry around a value of that thing anymore. Yes,
something happened, and it's a part of your past. But you forgive
somebody, and therefore it doesn't have a value of "good" or
"bad." It's forgiven. Something happens, and it's over.

Mira: So it becomes neutral?

Lisa's Higher Self: Yeah. And there is a huge amount of
connection that you're practicing. Again, it's not looking at it as
one person against another person. One against another creates
separation. Forgiving is really a pure practice of being connected.

What Lisa's Higher Self said is such an important key to understanding why forgiveness is so powerful. Forgiveness allows us to let go of the bitterness, anger, and blame that keep us separate. It allows us to connect with one another. Once our minds understand why complete forgiveness is so critical, we can let go more easily and without any reservations. Forgiveness is truly the path to Oneness.

Lisa told me that as Kelly was leaving that scene, she felt her energy—her spirit—move to "another level." I asked her Higher Self to tell me more:

Lisa's Higher Self: So when we move from life to life, or even from moment to moment, our spirit carries emotions with it. Pure spirit is the connection to this bigger love, with nothing else there. This other [emotional] stuff, it's heaviness. It's feeling sickness in the stomach. It's emptiness, loneliness, the feeling of disconnect. The more of that energy we can let go of, the higher the Spirit moves. It's moving closer to [Oneness], which from a human perspective seems bad. We don't want to let go of the person we are. But letting go of all [those negative emotions] is what gets you to be happier, more fulfilled, more connected to everything. By forgiving, you completely leave those negative energies.

Had Kelly left that life holding on to vindication energy—to hate, to the sense that it didn't seem fair—those energies would have to be balanced in another life. The visual I'm getting is a jar filled with white marbles. You could take along some black ones, representing that negative stuff. When you start your life, it's not completely obvious where the black marbles came from, or why you're holding on to them, but they're there. And maybe in time, with practice, through things like this session, you can figure them out, make sense of where those came from, and let go of them.

Mira: If Lisa can forgive, will that lessen the chances she will need to reconnect with these souls in a future life to work the forgiveness out?

Lisa's Higher Self: Yes. It's not that simple, though. I go back to the image of the white marbles. How many black marbles did you come into that life with? How many were there when you left? If you generated a lot of positivity in that life, it's easier to let go of any lingering negativity, to forgive. Because in the end, you can't fake it. It's a very honest moment as you're departing. The energy of that life can't lie about anything. It can't trick itself.

Lisa's Higher Self went on to stress how important it was for Lisa to forgive herself. A part of her actually blamed her body for the way that she had died as Kelly. If she hadn't been so attractive and desirable, Jim might not have murdered her. So she needed to forgive herself and her body from the life as Kelly. Also, Lisa needed to forgive herself for all the little things she had stored within her in this life. The Higher Self said that Lisa stored the negativity she holds against herself in a sort of "pile" within her. This pile created an emotional and energetic heaviness in Lisa.

The Higher Self made a very important point: There are two equally important aspects to the lesson of forgiveness. The first is forgiving those whom we perceive have harmed us. The second is forgiving ourselves. The two parts taken together allow for complete releasing of attachments and returning to love and Oneness. The Higher Self pointed out that Lisa was excellent at forgiving other people, as she held no grudges. But it advised her that she also must forgive herself. It is critical that, on the path of healing, we also release any self-blame and guilt we hold. (The exercise found on page 117 will detail how to do this.)

I asked the Higher Self to tell me more about Lisa's need to forgive herself:

Lisa's Higher Self: When spirits leave individual lives, they take some of the emotional energy from that life with them. While Kelly was able to forgive Jim, her brother, and her parents, the way she did it was to hold herself responsible. The deal kind of was, "I'll forgive them and take the blame." She didn't have to make that deal, but it's what happened in that moment. She felt somehow that her body had been at fault. That's the way her spirit made sense of the situation, and is how she was able to forgive everybody else so quickly. Those feelings carried over into this life.

In the course of our work together, Lisa severed the energetic connection to Kelly's experience. Self-forgiveness then allowed her to explore her relationship with her body. Once Lisa consciously recognized that Kelly's death had translated into a fear of having a desirable body, Lisa was ready to choose differently. She created a new deal for her body, mind, and spirit. This new way of being has allowed her to shift into a reality where she lives from a place of joy and appreciation for her body.

Suicide and Forgiveness

Suicide is a topic that comes up frequently, both in my regression sessions and from people I meet when they hear what I do. When we're considering forgiveness, it is important to discuss the spiritual consequences of taking one's own life.

Personally, I have never thought of committing suicide. Luckily for me, I have only heard stories of people who have attempted to take their lives—I haven't known anyone who has done so. However, the statistics clearly show that suicide is an escape route that many consider: The 2008 National Survey on Drug Use and Health revealed that there were 8.3 million adults in the United States alone who had serious thoughts of committing suicide in the past year. Another 2.3 million had made plans to commit suicide, and 1.1 million had actually attempted it. The World Health Organization states that, in some countries, suicide is among the top three leading causes of death for those 15 to 44 years of age. It estimates that globally there are between 10 and 20 million suicide attempts every year.

It is heart wrenching to read these numbers. Life is a sacred becoming, and by living we allow All That Is to expand and know itself through the unique perspective of our lives. Those of us who contemplate suicide do so because we're not able to see our own value in the eyes of the Creator. We are mired in doubts, fears, insecurities, and the overwhelming sense that there is no other choice. And yet that very act, the very ability to end one's physical existence, proves that we are in complete control. We control not only our bodies but also how we create and experience life.

One could argue that each of us has the right to commit suicide. After all, isn't the concept of free will a basic tenet of existence? Yes, it is. We are free to choose whether to live or die. However, there is a very important distinction between dying because one's time on the earthly plane has come to an end and purposefully choosing to take one's own life out of desperation.

A soul takes on a new incarnation because it is looking to create, learn, and experience certain lessons. The soul becomes enriched by the unique perspectives and experiences it creates during its time on Earth. While in physical form, the person's Higher Self knows very well when the soul's objectives have been accomplished. The very moment these lessons are learned, the soul is ready to return to a state of nonphysical being. Even the act of dying represents an opportunity to learn.

What most suicidal people don't see is that death is nothing more than a transformation, a transition from one state of being to another. The moment the spirit leaves the physical body, it returns to being limitless. It remembers why it chose the circumstances it did for that life, and it clearly sees how important it was to deal with those challenges rather than run away. It understands that by removing itself from physical reality, it has failed to fulfill the choices it made before incarnating. As a result, the soul usually reincarnates almost immediately into a situation that is similar to the one it escaped from.

When difficult emotions are plaguing us, then, the real answer is to release those emotions and forgive ourselves and others. The session I had with a client named Tamara exemplifies why it is important to heal emotionally through forgiveness.

Tamara was a very attractive woman who carried herself with grace and elegance. She grew up in Los Angeles as a child of immigrants, and her family had some difficulties. In her teenage years she discovered how easy it was to dull the pain of her fears, problems, and insecurities with drugs and alcohol. Her life began revolving around partying and rock and roll, and before she knew it, a few decades had passed by. With a very matter-of-fact attitude, she told me that she was a drug addict. She mentioned heroin, pot, and methadone, but said that they were things of the past.

A few months before coming to see me, her life had changed drastically. She had moved to another city, far away from her family and friends. Drugs and alcohol were no longer appealing to her. She was opening up to knowing herself and forgiving. She was excited about her growth and had scheduled a session with me because she wanted to make sense of it all.

During her regression, Tamara experienced a life where she was a young man who openly spoke his truth. He was brave and did not care what others thought. As a result of his beliefs, he was sentenced to life in prison. The prison was a dark, humid cave, and he could not imagine spending the rest of his life in that place. To escape, he used the chains that were around his arms to strangle himself.

When I spoke with Tamara's Higher Self, I asked some questions about suicide:

Mira: What happens to people when they commit suicide?

Tamara's Higher Self: They have to come back and live in "hell" and not commit suicide, to go through with the life. They have to go through their troubles, their problems. They have to learn. *You've got to learn.* You've got to go through it. You've got to pass through it. You've got to learn everything. And you've got to let it go. And that is the whole issue.

Mira: Would those issues be similar to the issues in the life where the person committed suicide, or would they be different?

Tamara's Higher Self: They will be different [on the surface], but the seed will be there. The same issue will be presented in a different form. It's just that the lesson has to be learned. And that lesson was not learned.

I asked the Higher Self why she had relived this particular life, and it replied, "Escape is not the answer. You cannot escape. You cannot think that you can escape your destiny, what you have to live through. It will follow you until you resolve it."

I then asked for steps on how Tamara could forgive herself and others, and move on with her life. "By looking at it," came the answer. "By feeling it. By living it. By resolving it. And then letting it go. That's what you do. Those are the steps."

The Higher Self acknowledged that learning the lesson of not escaping, but instead living her own truth, had not been easy for Tamara. It was encouraging, however, that she was on the right path now.

We live in a benevolent Universe. Our Creator is the essence of pure and unconditional love. Our Creator loves each one of us so much that, in its love, it allows us to *forget* how much we are loved. In its love for us, it allows us to experience ourselves as forgotten, neglected, and less than perfect, if we choose to know ourselves that way. But we are always loved and supported—whether we know it or not.

If it is true that we are timeless and we have all of eternity to reincarnate in as many lives as we need until we master our lessons to our own satisfaction, then the question becomes: Why commit suicide? Knowing that ending your life won't actually end your suffering—that it is almost 100 percent guaranteed that you'll choose to introduce yourself to circumstances that are similar to what you sought to avoid—it would make more sense to face those challenges as best you can right now.

In the darkest of times, when nothing else seems to be helping, give yourself courage and make this your mantra: "It won't always be the same." This is what my father, Manol Pasliev, used to say to me to cheer me up when things weren't looking good. He was so wise to give me hope by reminding me that change is the only permanent thing in our lives.

The soul is eternal. Even if suicide is something you never considered, I ask that you share these ideas with your friends and families. Together we can dispel the darkness of the taboo and bring light to the millions who need to hear that suicide is not the answer. But the power of this lesson goes beyond the direct shift in thinking about suicide. It allows us to feel empowered in every aspect of our lives.

The real key to transforming any displeasing situation you find yourself in is to forgive. Forgiveness lets you understand that you are not a victim of anything out there; you are not a person who is powerless over your own life. Allow yourself to know your magnificence. Know that you are very, very powerful in this moment —even if you're faced with circumstances you do not prefer, you have the power to change your life without harming yourself or others.

An Enlightened Approach to Forgiveness

When something disturbing takes place, it is only natural to want to express the hurt. I encourage you to do whatever you can to better the situation and heal from the pain, from taking action to stop the wrongdoing, to seeking professional help, to sharing and expressing your feelings in a way that will release them. But I also suggest something you may not have considered: Separate the action from the person who undertook it. Condemn the action but do not condemn the person who caused you harm. For when you condemn the person, you contribute to the experience of separation. Remember what Lisa's Higher Self said: "The Spirit has no purpose to punish a part of itself. And we're all part of each other." Forgiveness is a clearing tool that allows you to return to Oneness and to the place of peace within you.

Release the pain, right any wrongs you can, but do not seek to fight or attack the person. Instead, seek to understand her motivation. Know that at its core, any wrongdoing stems from a feeling of powerlessness—the inability to create what we desire without hurting ourselves and others. The person who wronged you is also a soul that is simply here on Earth to learn. Find it in you to see how small and scared she is, and how she too is holding on to stories filled with lack of forgiveness. Understand what motivated her not so that you can find excuses for what she did, but so you can really feel compassion toward her.

Once you find compassion, the person who wronged you is no longer a big, scary monster to be fought. She is simply a small, scared child who does not know how truly powerful she is. Once you have compassion for someone, you are only an inch away from fully forgiving her . . . and then simply letting go. Forgive not because the other person deserves to be forgiven but because you deserve to be at peace. Forgive because you love yourself more than the need to be "right."

Now I'd like to share with you three short phrases from my teacher Dolores Cannon. The power of these words, when stated with intent, is immense:

I forgive you. I release you. I let you go.

To forgive yourself, you can add another part: *I forgive myself.* Thus, the mantra becomes:

I forgive myself. I forgive you. I release you. I let you go.

Commit these words to memory. Make them your prayer and use them every day in every situation. If something disturbing comes up, don't let it sit in you, attracting more and more of the same experiences. Instantly, speak this little mantra and choose to release and let go in the moment.

Another prayer I love for its power to shift energetic universes was given to me by Tabaash, a spiritual teacher who is channeled by Blair Styra. I use this prayer with my clients who need to forgive themselves and others. If forgiveness is the issue you are currently working on, write this prayer on a piece of paper and carry it with you in your wallet. From time to time pull it out and read it. Even just seeing the prayer when you open your wallet, knowing that it is always with you, will anchor you in your preferred reality.

This is Tabaash's Special Prayer:

From the Lord God of my being
I empty myself, mind, body and spirit,
Of all that limits me,
Of all I am attached to, that does not serve me
Of all I am addicted to, that does not profit me.
I ask for forgiveness from all people I have hurt
In my life, in any life, in any way at all.
I forgive all those who have hurt me
In my life, in any life, in any way at all.
And I forgive myself for all the ways I have hurt myself,
For all the times I did not pay attention
In my life, in any life, in any way at all.
And I now choose to be at peace.
Always
In all ways
So be it.

Exercise: The Forgiveness Process

This exercise is helpful when there is someone in your life who you feel has wronged you. The first step is to explore other life connections you've had with this person, to try to understand where his motivations were coming from. Once you understand the tapestry that you have weaved with this person through the different lives, it's much easier to extend forgiveness.

The first part of this process requires you to regress yourself. To do so, you can use the regression script that is included in Appendix A. You can either record yourself reading the script—and then play it back—or you can have a close and trusted friend be your regressionist and read the script for you. You can also choose to use the guided regression recording that is part of my CD set, *Healing Through Past-Life Regression . . . and Beyond* (see the Further Resources section).

When you're ready to explore your past lives, give yourself at least 40 minutes of uninterrupted time. Have your journal nearby so that you can reflect and share afterward. Before you begin, set the intention to explore a life that will help you understand the challenge you are having.

Play the recording and trust that you'll be presented with exactly what you need. If the regression brings up a cathartic experience, allow yourself the time to integrate what is revealed. If tears come up, allow for the expression of those emotions. Following the regression, you may want to journal or otherwise take the time to reflect, take a bath, or drink some water. Listen to your intuition and be gentle with yourself. You may choose to do the regression and the next step of the process as described below in the same day or on different days. Whichever you choose, simply trust your inner guidance.

Next, create an environment for you to continue this important work. You may want to light a candle, burn some incense, play soft music, or hold your favorite crystal. Sit somewhere comfortable and peaceful. Give yourself at least 20 minutes. Make sure you have the two prayers given previously in this chapter—the forgiveness mantra and Tabaash's Special Prayer. Take your time as you feel and see every step of this process.

First, close your eyes and imagine that the unconditional love of Source is entering powerfully through the top of your head. It cleanses your mind and your thought patterns of the need to hold on to old stories. Feel this Divine love going through your entire body, releasing the memories stored in the cells of your body and cleansing your energy field. Through your imagination, concentrate this unconditional love of Source around your heart. Feel it infusing your heart. Feel it healing your heart. Say out loud, "I forgive myself. I forgive you, _____." In the blank, insert your own name. Say it with intent. You may choose to say it a few more times until you deeply and profoundly feel within your heart that you have forgiven yourself.

Now, imagine the person you want to forgive standing in front of you. Feel how the powerful beam of Divine light and love extends from your heart and connects with his. If there is something that you would like to say to him to bring closure, speak the words. Express your compassion out loud. Thank him for bringing you to a better place in your life, for teaching you how strong you are. Then, take a deep breath and say out loud:

I forgive you. I release you. I let you go.

Speak every word with intent. Repeat them several times if you would like.

Now, see this person being absorbed into the Light—disappearing into the Light. Take a deep breath in, and feel the clarity and expansion that has been created within you.

To complete this process, slowly recite Tabaash's Special Prayer out loud. As you speak each word, mean it. When done, take a deep breath in and know that it is so. This is your new state of being—freer and clearer.

Forgiveness Is Freedom

While writing this chapter, I had a session with a woman named Maria. She saw herself surrounded by her soul group and, for the first time in her life, felt how deeply she belongs. Tears rolled down her cheeks as she saw how much she is loved. Maria's soul group told her that her only purpose in life is to just be herself, to radiate love to those around her. Unfortunately, her unwillingness to forgive was standing in the way of Maria shining her light brightly, and it was also preventing her from shedding her excess weight. The need to forgive was conveyed to her with a great emphasis.

The soul group said, "You know how to forgive. When you forgive, you release the light within you. By holding on to [past wrongs], you block your creativity. You block your own abilities and knowledge. When you forgive, you will open up the light for everyone else.

"Once you forgive, all barriers and blocks will be released. Forgiveness changes the vibration. Higher vibrations open up space and possibilities. Anger and hatred are gray, dense energies. Forgiveness releases. It cleanses. When you forgive, you change your energy and you glow. Also, you change your relationships with people. You become free to go forward. You are no longer attached to people and circumstances. If you have not forgiven them yet, you are dragging them along like chains around you. When you forgive, space and new opportunities open up because you shift to a new dimension, and you release yourself as if you're flying with balloons, just like in the movie *Up!*" (This is an animated movie about a man who turns his house into an airship lifted off the ground by thousands of helium balloons.)

My earlier sessions with Lisa also gave me a deeper understanding of why forgiveness is so important. Lisa's experience as Kelly revealed to me that forgiveness is one of the most important spiritual practices we have. Being unwilling to forgive keeps us away from being at one with All That Is and ascending in our soul growth. Forgiveness is a clearing tool on our path to Oneness. It creates a sense of deep peace and frees our creativity, allowing for the greatest potential in our lives.

One of the new possibilities that appears when we are free of anger, blame, and hatred is the opportunity to play with time. The knowledge that existence is simultaneous brings with it some very interesting implications about what's possible in life. We will explore these topics in the chapter that follows. This information will open doorways to new dimensions in your mind—it's as if you will find yourself in a world of wonders, and you will begin to relate to everything in a new way.

CHAPTER 7

YOU CAN PLAY WITH TIME

You and I process the occurrence of events in our lives in terms of linear time. We think of things that happened yesterday, a month ago, or a year ago as "the past." We make vacation plans and schedule our appointments for specific moments in "the future." This is only logical. We all know that time unfolds as a progression from past to future, right? This is one of the very few things that all of humanity can agree on. So if we all believe that time flows progressively, and we all assume that this is an un-disputed fact, then how is it possible that time is also simultaneous?

Physicists tell us that the past, present, and future are the same one moment. Albert Einstein supported the simultaneity of existence and rejected the separation we experience from one moment to another. When a close friend of his, Michele Besso, passed away, Einstein wrote this in a letter to Besso's family: "Now he has departed from this strange world a little ahead of me. That means nothing. People like us, who believe in physics, know that the distinction between past, present, and future is only a stubbornly persistent illusion."

Einstein's words encourage us to understand that past events are not gone and forever lost in the ether, but exist and happen in the now moment. Similarly, all future events are already here as well. What we experience as an objective flow of time is simply a mirage. Source does not experience time; however, we on the earthly plane experience it as very structured and rigid in its unfolding. How do we reconcile the two?

Time does not need to be existent *or* nonexistent. Although from the Earth perspective it seems exclusive, the nature of time is actually *inclusive*. Time is both simultaneous *and* linear. It exists not only in time, but also in no time. Moreover, it exists in the space between the two—where the existence of time varies, depending on how you look at it. The point of view from which you observe events determines how you perceive the flow of those events in time.

Time is a construct that our collective consciousness has agreed upon—it's one of the rules of the game here on Earth. It serves as a tool for creation, because it helps define the borders of our playground. Simultaneously, each one of us creates time in our own consciousness. By doing this, we reinforce the collective agreement on time. That said, all of us fall out of time on occasion. We say, "Time flies when you're having fun." Such experiences confirm that time is a filter we impose on our awareness.

When we play with a child, read an enjoyable book, or have a great conversation with a friend, the construct of time seems to fall away. In those instances we exist completely in the present moment, focused on the joy and fulfillment of the now. We're so concentrated on what makes us feel good that we create little or no time. Then, once that activity is done, we look at the clock and say, "Look what time it is!" At that moment we quickly fall back into our collective understanding of time.

Time and Creation

As rigid and limiting as time is, it also serves a great purpose. It allows us to experience the process of creation. Think of all those instances when your heart's desire was taking its time in coming to you. How frustrating and discouraging that was! Of course, it would be fabulous to have every wish fulfilled in an instant, right?

In those dimensions of existence where time is not a factor, creation *is* instantaneous. I can assure you that your soul has created universes in an instant. In those dimensions between lives, when we are in spirit form, we can merely think of something and we have it. But in this earthly dimension, instantaneous creation takes a true master. It takes a maestro to skillfully combine the pieces of vision, desire, guidance, action, and surrender into one creation. I invite you to really ponder the importance of these words. You chose to incarnate in a place with great restrictions—space and time being only two of them. It's a place filled with potential for palpable negativity, too. Yet you came here because you knew your strengths and your abilities. You are a true alchemist who, through the force of love, finds the way around any limitation. Give yourself a nod of recognition. You are doing absolutely great, no matter what your circumstances are.

Once we recognize how truly powerful we are, the process of creation becomes a pleasant journey. Space and time are gifts to be treasured. In the space and time between desire and manifestation, you become the dream. You become the reality you dreamed of. You become a vibrational match to your desire through every encounter in your life. Through every interaction with every person, through the experience of every event, you constantly clarify for yourself what you prefer and choose to manifest. You become more of yourself, and that is the purpose of your existence.

In the dimension of your soul, all past, present, and future blend into a timeless now. At that level, consciousness experiences all of its different creations in the same one moment, each one from a different perspective. Your soul is not subject to space and time. Space and time exist within the consciousness that creates them.

You have decided to project yourself into this particular moment on Earth because of the exciting changes that are transpiring. People are awakening through the study of metaphysical ideas and the exploration of their own consciousness. We are no longer reaching for the Light in sporadic, singular cases, like little fireflies blinking in the night. Millions and millions of us are openly exploring our spirituality. A dimensional shift in our collective consciousness is taking place. We came to life on Earth in this very moment to partake and assist in this creative exuberance.

Our Newtonian understanding of time and space—which says that time and space are independent aspects of objective reality—has served to enforce the notion of separateness for centuries. But these are different times. We are moving into a reality of greater harmony, love, and well-being, where we operate from a conscious recognition of our connectedness right here on Earth. We are choosing to step outside of old limitations and become more expanded, intentionally seeking to understand and nurture our relationship with Source. That is why it is important to give ourselves a new interpretation of our experience of time on Earth—so we can more easily erase the mental borders of our separateness. When we become attuned to the Oneness of all, we naturally allow the rigidity of time to soften. Time becomes like clay—we can stretch, compress, mold, and play with it because this lets us know ourselves as the powerful creators that we are.

A Shift in Thinking

Up to this moment in the human journey, time has been a rule of the game of separation. It has helped enhance our experience of separateness from All That Is. By imposing the filter of linearity on our consciousness, we have removed ourselves from the simultaneous and instantaneous nature of Source. This separation-based approach to creating reality is a valid approach; by imposing time on ourselves, we have greatly added to the ways in which Source knows itself. But as with all things, growth occurs through changes in perspective.

We are beginning to recognize a strong yearning within us—a yearning for growth, expansion, and connectedness. We want to experience the feeling of being unconditionally loved and supported. We yearn to return to the One, and to know it as if for the first time. In order to do this while still in our physical bodies, we must leave behind traditional thought patterns about time and space. Time is not a given, so see it for the tool that it is. Know that it originates within your consciousness; as such, you are *its* master. Begin to question all your beliefs about time. Allow the sharp and clearly defined edges of "time" to soften.

This one simple but very profound shift in thinking can make a big difference. Knowing that you can play with time will empower you, allowing you to know yourself as the creator you are. When you accept this new definition of time, your life will become magical. The boundaries of what is possible will expand. When you do this, you will begin experiencing the Oneness of All That Is and the simultaneous existence of all things.

There is something so exciting and wonderful about the moments when causally unrelated events come together perfectly in time. Synchronicities are a representation of the holographic nature of the Universe—where everything is the same one thing, experienced from different points of view by different aspects of All That Is. Synchronicities are our reminder that all things exist, develop, and manifest in the same one moment of time. The more we live in the present moment, the more frequent our experience of synchronicity becomes.

Recently I flew from New York City to San Diego to meet some friends. On the morning of my arrival, my friends were driving down from Los Angeles. I had no idea what time they would get there; we just said we'd meet after we all got to the hotel. When my plane parked at the gate, I sent them a text message telling them I had landed and asking them if they had arrived. Ten minutes later, as I was making my way toward the airport exit, my phone rang.

"I just reached for my phone to call you and saw your message," my friend said. "Are you in a taxi yet?"

"No," I said. "I'm on my way to catch one."

"Believe it or not, we are a couple of minutes away from the airport. We can just swing by and get you."

Such synchronicities have become the hallmark of my life. I'm sure you have more than a few good stories of moments when life effortlessly put the pieces together for you. It is astounding to think how brilliant the organizing force of the Universe is. Just in this simple example, there were so many parts that had to come together in unison. My friends had to leave Los Angeles at just the right time; the traffic on the freeway had to be just right; my flight had to leave New York without delays; my friends had to be only a few minutes away from the airport; and my friend had to call me before I caught a taxi. Had I planned for these events to coincide, I doubt I would have done it so well. What a fascinating orchestration this one small event required!

Every moment of our lives is just as brilliantly orchestrated. Everything exists in this now moment to support you and enhance the person you are. Know that the whole Universe is conspiring to give you exactly what you need in the moment that you need it. All you have to do is trust and pay attention. Trust that what you need will be there at the perfect time. Also, listen to your intuition and stay aware so that you can recognize the information— the help and the answers—when they present themselves to you.

Perfect Timing

One way to play with time is to take your focus off of clock-based "time" and place it on the concept of "timing." It starts with a reconsideration of the belief that things need to happen at a specific time. In the big scheme of things, the timing of any event is always perfect—regardless of whether it matches your expectations.

Being "on time" used to be very important to me. In fact, I used to pride myself on being punctual. I thought timeliness showed that I was a serious, reliable person. I also thought that being on time for meetings expressed the respect I had for the person I was meeting with. Needless to say, I used to get irritated when people were late for our appointments. In those days I also used to wear a watch. In fact, I had quite a few of them. Some were casual and some were elegant; I wore them like jewelry.

Then, something happened. I'm not quite sure what it was, but suddenly I became the exact opposite. I became the kind of person I had disliked before! I was late for every meeting and for every event. I no longer wore a watch. (Frankly, I have no idea where all my beloved watches went.) Thankfully, every time I met with friends or family I had the convenient (and true) excuse that I was late because of work. Even though no one ever scolded me for being late, I was living with an almost permanent anxiety. I was always in a rush and feeling guilty for making other people wait for me.

Previously, being on time created rigidity and anxieties of its own. It prevented me from fully experiencing the pleasure of every moment because I had to be so mindful of the time. However, being stressed out because I was late and out of time was not a good place to be either. I knew that there had to be a third way—a way that allowed me to relax into the joy of every moment and still be on time for all my meetings.

No sooner did I ask my Higher Self for help with this than my understanding of time began to expand. I recognized that time is not something outside of me that I need to measure myself against. *I* am the one who creates time in my consciousness. Therefore, I can manipulate it. Because my creation of time is naturally synchronized with everyone else's creation of time, I knew I had an internal clock I could trust. Because the time mechanism was already in place within me, all I had to do was direct it differently.

I placed my intent on having an exact timing. I chose to fall out of *time* and fall into *timing*. I crafted a mantra for myself: *My timing is always perfect. My timing is always right.* I began repeating this affirmation to myself. As I chose to affirm the truth of it, the world confirmed its validity everywhere I turned.

Now I experience every moment to its fullest. On the occasions that I'm late for meetings, my timing is still perfect. Often the other person is delayed as well! That is exactly what took place on a recent afternoon. I was to have an important meeting that

I anticipated with excitement and a bit of anxiety. I could only schedule an hour for the appointment, so I didn't have any time to spare in getting to the meeting place. Being my wonderful self, I took all the time in the world to get ready. When I left the house, I looked at the clock on my mobile phone and with horror recognized that I would be at least 30 minutes late. I frantically increased my pace as I walked toward the subway station.

A second later my phone rang, and it was the person I was to meet with. He told me that *he* was running late, and wouldn't be there for approximately 30 minutes. After we hung up, I slowed my pace. With relief and a little cheek, I reminded myself, "You see, Mira! My timing is always perfect. My timing is always right."

The very next day I had another opportunity to create magic around the idea of time. I was on my way to another meeting, and sure enough, I was running late. The meeting started at 9:00 A.M., and I was going to be there by 9:15 A.M. at the earliest. Again, it was an important meeting, and I really wanted to be on time.

As I left my building and headed to the subway station, I reminded myself that I create my reality. I told myself that I am able to compress time and use much less of it to travel than would normally be needed to get to the meeting place. Rather than getting there 15 minutes late, which was the trajectory I was on, I decided I wanted to be there 15 minutes *early*. That meant I had to accommodate for 30 additional minutes that I did not physically have. I simply and clearly directed myself to be there at 8:45 A.M. I reminded myself that there is no causality and continuity between separate, distinct "now" moments.

While traveling to my destination, I avoided looking at the clocks that were all around me. That way I couldn't confirm whether my plan was working, and didn't have to deal with any possible doubt. But when I arrived I looked at my phone, and voila—it was 8:45 A.M. I felt such a sweet sense of triumph and success in that moment.

Exercise: Time Yourself

This exercise is unlike the others given in this book. It is meant to give you your own unique experience, instead of putting you through a process. Rather than giving you steps, I want to engage your intuition and your inner guidance.

Start by asking yourself in what areas of your life you would like to improve your timing. Then use my little mantra, *My timing is always perfect. My timing is always right.* Repeat it over and over. The key to experiencing your ability to manipulate time is to trust yourself. Once you have directed yourself to have perfect timing, it will be so. Then watch how your new belief about your timing becomes the organizing force of your life. It will simultaneously assure that you are punctual, and that you have time for everything you need.

Travel, as exemplified by earlier stories in this chapter, is an easy way to begin experimenting with the manipulation of time.

I also want to encourage you to stop wearing a watch. For those of you who are deeply attached to your timepieces and for whom such an idea borders on insanity, try going watch-free for a day. It will give you the opportunity to acquaint yourself with your inner timing and to open up to trusting it. You don't need to worry about knowing what time it is. Your mobile phone will not let you forget, and if it does, there are many helpful strangers who would gladly tell you the time if you ask. The reward for not having a watch on your wrist is the experience of liberation. You will free yourself from the confines of rigidity and allow your natural self to follow its instincts—to easily flow with the energy of its timeless Source.

Because time is an aspect of all of our experiences, you can apply the idea of having an excellent timing to anything you set out to accomplish. It could be as small as showing up at your favorite coffee shop to find there is no line, or roasting the Thanksgiving turkey without a timer. You could apply this principle to buying and selling stocks at the precise moments that would assure that you receive the greatest profit. Significant decisions—such as the launch of a new product or the sale of the family business—will also benefit from the intention for perfect timing.

Approach the manipulation of time with the playfulness and curiosity of a child. It is a fun way to know yourself as the powerful creator that you are.

The Power of the Present

If indeed Einstein is right that the distinction between past, present, and future is only a stubbornly present illusion, why don't our senses confirm it? The answer lies in the way we have been brought up to process the world. We've been conditioned to think consequentially since infants. If you spend more than a few minutes around a child who is starting to explore the world, you'll hear their parents say, "Don't do that, because . . ." over and over. The consequences are always clear: *If you do this, a definite something will result.* We are given a cause-and-effect frame of thinking. So from the time we start learning language and existing in the world, we are taught to arrange information linearly. We see how one event flows into the next. The belief in cause and effect expands as we grow up and become more involved with the world. It becomes natural for us to think that what *was* creates what *is*.

Now that you have the ability as a grownup to consciously choose how you see the world, I invite you to shake loose the chain of causation. Consider this: The past does not create the present. *The present creates the past and the future.*

The present is the only moment in which you hold the power to manifest. As Seth says, "The present is the point of power." You are not at the mercy of unfortunate bygone events that cannot be changed. There is no connection between moments. All the moments of your past and all the moments of your future exist simultaneously within the present. When you look back, your mind—as directed by your beliefs—sifts through events and chooses those that fit into the outcome you are looking to affirm. How you presently feel changes the nuances, details, and lessons of your life stories. Every different read of an event is a different reality.

No story of your past is set in stone. You are constantly reorganizing your past based on your present interpretation of it. We say that memories change and fade. What we don't realize is that every memory, as a thought we are having now, is *our interpretation of a possible past*. Similarly, every thought you have in the present alters your path through the possible futures you are to experience.

But how is it possible that the present is not the effect of the past? After all, everyone knows that if we put our hand on a hot stove we will get burned. Don't we? In truth, we experience having our hand on a hot stove in the "now" moment. The next "now" moment we experience will depend on our conditioning. Given the reality of our hand on the hot stove, two other realities may follow. One is a reality in which we develop a burn on our hand. In the second reality, we don't get burned. It is our set of beliefs, thoughts, and feelings—as they exist in the moment—that instantly decides which reality we experience as our future. We can choose between either possibility, but the choice is never conscious. It occurs almost instantly.

In the moment of choice, we are simply shifting into a reality that is most closely aligned with the beliefs and expectations we already have. When we change our overall thoughts on what is possible in the different areas of our lives, however, things change. The next time we're presented with a choice of different possible realities, we will naturally orient ourselves to a new possibility— one that is aligned with our new set of beliefs and expectations.

The hot stove is an example of an *unconscious* choice between different realities; now bring your attention to the moments in life when you make *conscious* choices about your reality. That is where you can begin to practice breaking the expectation of causation between events.

Because the cause of an event and its end result exist in the same moment, you can create your reality by choosing either as your starting point. You can start with cause, knowing that it will lead you to a certain effect. For example, you can work hard and know that your efforts will lead to you getting a promotion, which would result in the higher income you desire. Or you can begin with the result and then draw to yourself reasons that reinforce the result. For example, people say that they are going to be happy only when something changes in their life, such as getting the job they want or attracting the partner they dream of. Shifting into the desired reality will occur much faster if they already live from the place of the end result, feeling within every fiber of their being that they are happy right now.

You don't need permission—or a particular set of past events—to be the highest version of yourself you can imagine in this moment. When you break the need for causation, you become the vibration of the effect you desire; no intermediary steps are required. If you can imagine it, you are it. Happening and becoming exist simultaneously, side by side. Remind yourself often that the present moment is the moment of your true power. When you know—really *know*—this, you will begin to very powerfully claim the future of your highest good. You will shift through realities very quickly, consciously directing yourself on the path of your becoming.

If there's no such thing as one predetermined future, how is it possible for psychics to make predictions? The answer lies within the present. All of time, just like all of space, exists in the present moment. Therefore, what psychics sense is the present moment. They read the energies existing right now. Behind every question, every dream, and every problem is a certain set of beliefs, intentions, hopes, and actions that have been built up over time. That energy is what tells a psychic which realities are possible for you.

Most people approach speaking with a psychic believing that there is only one, already-determined future. In fact, there are many possible futures that exist, depending on the energy that has been accumulating. We people are creatures of habit. Therefore, unless we make an intentional choice and take action in a new direction, we will arrive at the destination we're headed to. Sometimes, speaking with a psychic and hearing something that is not to our liking is the way we subconsciously guide ourselves in a new direction. A single choice can open up a new field of possibilities that were remote or improbable before.

Consider speaking with a psychic as an exploration of possibilities. When you see the psychic as a person who can sense your issues and your vibration, you retain your own power. When you take that approach, you don't have to wait and see, hoping that the psychic is right or wrong. You understand that you're hearing someone's counsel, but you're still required to make your own decisions about how you want your life to be.

A New Perspective on Patience

How many times have you been told to have patience, or heard that "patience is a virtue"? Often we hear these sentiments when we're not getting what we want.

We believe that it is noble and admirable to persevere in the face of disappointment and delay. We are encouraged not to express our negative feelings of annoyance and anger. We observe the painful passage of time, wishing, hoping, and praying that things would change for the better—fast. And when we show or recognize how impatient we feel, we inflict even more pain by judging ourselves as impatient. The belief in patience has created so much unnecessary agony and suffering for us!

I'd like to share a new perspective here—one that is liberating rather than judgmental. I invite you to give up patience and instead seek to live in the present moment. When you live in the now, you can trust that things are the way they need to be. This is not because you become resigned and give up dreaming of a better future; instead, you allow things to be as they are without rebelling against them. You know that every situation is there to serve you. You are a powerful creator, and no moment of your time on Earth has come together by chance. You attract every situation, even conditions that you dislike, because they help you grow and expand in understanding. Use this kind of reasoning to make peace with where you are.

As Lucile and Jean-Pierre Garnier-Malet say in their book *Change Your Future Through Time Openings*, "A migrating bird knows that better living lies in enjoying the present while at the same time anticipating a better future on another continent."

You may ask, "What about the change that I desire?" Things *will* change. They always do. As the Greek philosopher Heraclitus said, "Change is the only constant." I love this quotation because it conveys that nothing in life is permanent *except* change. Whether things change for the worse or for the better depends on you. It is your interpretation of the events that gives them a positive or negative coloration. Because it is guaranteed that all events will change, your only task is to choose how you judge the value of the new circumstances—whether you give them the label "good" or "bad." But if you return to the trust that everything transpires for the sole purpose of benefiting you, this is an easy choice to make.

Knowing that all is as it needs to be, and knowing that change is inevitable, all you're left with is the present moment. You can choose to make the most of it. Your life is worth living and enjoying, even when things are not ideal. When you focus on how much time it has taken and continues to take for things to change, you become more aware of the passing of time. That awareness gives you the impression that time is dragging on endlessly, and thus creates the experience of *more* time. When you decide to dive into the moment and have fun, you stop experiencing the passing of time in the same way.

Previously, when you constantly reminded yourself that things needed to change and asked why change was so slow to come, you experienced more of the trickling of time. It is the experience of the seemingly unbearable and unending stretch of time that creates the issue of impatience. Think about all the times you've stood by a microwave watching the dial, counting the seconds until your meal was heated. The last few seconds always seem to take the longest! It feels as if each one lasts an eternity.

Put all issues of impatience to rest by simply living in the moment. When you are thoroughly present, awake, and aware, you will see that you have every reason to marvel at your life and be in awe of it—including the messy bits. In any moment, do what will give you the greatest amount of pleasure, and you're guaranteed to experience the speeding up of time. As a result, change will take place faster.

The very first time I consciously turned my attention toward pleasure and experienced time speed up, I was waiting for a taxi. I had just returned home from an exhausting one-day trip to Asheville, North Carolina. To get back to New York City I had to first fly through Charlotte, North Carolina, where I had a long layover. The flight to New York was full, and I had a middle seat. The gentlemen on either side of me struck up a lively conversation, bonding over their shared irritation at the prices of bridge tolls and good tomatoes. You can imagine that by the time the plane landed at La Guardia Airport—well after midnight—I was very ready to get home.

But when I got to the taxi stand, the line was huge. It seemed as if everyone who was on that flight had lined up for a cab. Because it was late at night, the cars were arriving to pick up passengers once every 5 to 10 minutes. As I stood there, I went through all the reasons why this shouldn't be happening to me. I was already tired from my trip. I had to wake up very early the next morning. And I had a stressful day at the office ahead of me, with a big deal about to close.

Everyone around me in the line was impatiently shifting from side to side. Many were openly expressing how unpleasant the situation was. Knowing that being grumpy wouldn't get me home any sooner, I chose to think differently. I remembered that all the people around me were part of *my* experience, and that I can choose my own reality. I also knew that, in order to compress my experience of time, I needed to occupy my mind with something that would grasp my attention completely. I had a book that was interesting to me, so I pulled it out and began reading, opting to ignore all the displeased people around me.

I barely finished one page of the book when I looked up. To my surprise, there was only one person ahead of me in line, and she was walking toward her taxi. My cab was right behind hers. I was astonished.

"What happened to the 50 people who were in line ahead of me?" I asked myself. Before I'd begun reading, it had seemed it would take at least an hour to get to the front of the line. I'm a fast reader, so reading one page doesn't take long for me. Everything felt very surreal. I had created an experience where the line lasted a few brief minutes, rather than the hour I'd previously calculated. Perhaps a fleet of cars descended in a very short amount of time and whisked away everyone ahead of me, and I'm fine with that explanation. What I hope you take away from this story—and apply to your life—is the recognition that it is indeed possible to manipulate your *experience* of time.

When you focus on the present moment and engage in something engrossing, you create less awareness of the passing of time. In that way you create *less* time, because time is not an absolute. The change you're looking to experience happens faster. And who needs patience when you're enjoying yourself and time just keeps flying by?

The Seed Is Planted

I hope that by now the seed of knowledge that the past, present, and future all exist in the present moment has been planted in your mind. As Jesus said, "The kingdom of God is as if a man should scatter seed upon the ground, and should sleep and rise night and day, and the seed should sprout and grow, he knows not how" (Mark 4:26–27).

Your understanding of the simultaneity of time and its implications for your life will develop at whatever pace is appropriate for you. Just like a stone that has been thrown into a pond, the vibrations of this knowledge will create ripples in your consciousness. This information will affect and alter every aspect of your life at whatever rate and in whichever way serves you best.

Now let's explore a different seed I'd like to plant within you: how changing our beliefs about health allows us to shift into a reality of well-being.

CHAPTER 8

YOU CAN HEAL YOUR BODY

I love the story of the near-death experience (NDE) of my beloved friend Anita Moorjani. It is told in her riveting book, *Dying to Be Me,* which I encourage you to read. Anita's NDE powerfully teaches us that we have the ability to choose the direction of our lives as well as the parallel realities that correspond to those choices.

After four years of living with Hodgkin's lymphoma, Anita's body was beginning to die of organ failure, and she was given only 36 hours to live. She was drifting in and out of consciousness, and felt her spirit leave her body. In this disembodied state, she felt surrounded by a profound, unconditional love. She also experienced total clarity: she knew why she had the disease, what roles her family members played, and why she had come into this current incarnation in the first place.

At that moment, Anita understood each human being's immense potential to create life. She was given the choice to continue into the nonphysical realm, allowing her body to die, or to return to life and teach her fellow human beings how magnificent we all are and that we have the power to create heaven on Earth. Anita was concerned that if she returned to her physical body, she would continue to be sick. In response, she was shown that her decision to live or die would determine her reality. If she chose to live, her body would heal very quickly. If she chose to die, her body would die of organ failure. This is how Anita has described it:

> I was made to understand that, as tests had been taken for my organ functions (and the results were not out yet), that if I chose life, the results would show that my organs were functioning normally. If I chose death, the results would show organ failure as the cause of death, due to cancer. I was able to change the outcome of the tests by my choice!
>
> Time seems to have a completely different meaning on that side. What I felt was that all possibilities exist simultaneously—it just depends which one you choose. Sort of like being in an elevator, where all the floors of a building exist, but you can choose which floor to get off on. So if all the future possibilities exist for me to choose from, then I assume all the past scenarios exist, too. So depending on which future possibility I choose, that will also determine which past automatically comes with it (I chose life, so it affected the past, choosing the appropriate test result for the organ function). . . . When I was being presented the choice, I actually saw a vision of my lab report, which said, on the heading: *Diagnosis: Organ Failure.* Then on the body of the report: *Death due to organ failure caused by Hodgkin's lymphoma.* When I actually saw the report after coming back, the sheet of paper looked almost identical, and the heading matched word for word: *Diagnosis: Organ Failure;* however, the body read: *There is no evidence of organ failure.* I actually got goosebumps looking at that report, knowing what it could have read. . . .
>
> I discovered that since I'd realized who I really was and understood the magnificence of my true self, if I chose to go back to life, my body would heal rapidly—not in months or weeks, but in days! I *knew* that the doctors wouldn't find a trace of cancer if I chose to go back to my body! . . . I understood that my body is only a reflection of my internal state. If my inner self were aware of its greatness and connection with All That Is, my body would soon reflect that and heal rapidly.

Anita's beliefs about life and who she is were so dramatically transformed through her experience on the Other Side that every cell in her body very quickly reflected her new understanding.

She'd had tumors the size of lemons throughout her body when she was admitted in the hospital. Within days of coming out of the coma, the tumors had shrunk at least 70 percent. And five weeks after entering the hospital, she was released to go home because there was no evidence of cancer in her body. A week later, Anita celebrated her birthday—and her new life—by going out to dinner with family at her favorite restaurant.

John's Instantaneous Healing

Anita Moorjani's rapid recovery came after she connected with the love of All That Is and understood that she *is* that same love. That's how quick and instantaneous physical healing can be! It is not necessary for each of us to die in order to return to life healed. The regression sessions that I conduct provide the environment for the healing of the body to take place. John is a good example of this.

Speaking with his Higher Self, I asked whether John had any organs that needed healing. The reply came that he was healthy at the moment, but that he had "a lot of choices to make." The Higher Self said that John would do anything he needed to do in this life to learn and teach the lesson of understanding he had come to learn and teach—even get sick.

Hearing this affirmed for me that illness is never caused by bad genes or bad luck, and it is never random. Illness is simply the opportunity to grow. When a soul chooses for the body to experience distress, it is doing so to learn through the challenge. When the ego is disconnected—when we ignore the signs, the prompting, the whispers of our soul to fulfill its plan—the Higher Self may be forced to orchestrate an illness or an accident to get the point across. Challenges make us look for answers. They have us search for the reasons why, put our life in perspective, and hopefully learn the lessons we've been resisting. Illness is a hard way to learn, but oftentimes a drastic measure is the only path left. If we're too busy running in circles in our minds to open up to guidance and direction, then the Higher Self will have no choice but to resort to extreme measures.

Continuing the conversation with John's Higher Self, I was told that his only physical issue concerned his eyes. I asked whether it were possible for us to heal them right now, and the answer was yes. After the session I discovered that John had a known issue with his left eye. While his right eye was fine, he had left his left contact lens in too long and there was some damage. I requested that it be healed, and John's Higher Self replied that it was.

The conversation that the Higher Self and I had on the subject of John's health lasted all but a couple of minutes. After our session, John sent me this e-mail:

> Just wanted to give you a quick update. After our session I went to the eye doctor, and my eyes were about the same as usual—no wound was found, though. I went back yesterday for a little checkup. Ha! Despite my resistance to giving up contact lenses, would you believe my eyes have actually gotten *better?* When he told me the new numbers, I thought back to the healing portion of our session. Thank you!

Your body knows how to heal and restore itself; you just need to provide the environment for it to do so. I believe that John already had the conviction that instantaneous healing was possible, and that one could be healed through unconventional means. Because his session with me was so profound, he simply accepted that his eye was healed from the wound. Note that we didn't even work on improving his eyesight—the Higher Self only worked on removing the damage caused by his contact lens. Yet, because John accepted that his eye was healed, the power of that new belief transcended the specific ailment and improved the overall well-being of his eyes.

Exercise: Do You Believe in Instant Healing?

Do you believe you can be healed? More important, do you believe you can be *instantly* healed? The answers to these two questions—especially the second one—are critical to the healing itself. Whatever the type of healing, be it a session with me, the work of other healers, or the work of doctors trained in Western medicine, any modality is simply a tool. The healing modality provides the proper environment for your return to good health. The healing itself, however, grows out of the convictions a person has. Therefore, if we transcend our beliefs about what is possible for the body, then the path to wellness is present.

If you are seeking a physical healing, I recommend you begin by changing your attitudes around your body's ability to heal—and how quickly it can do so. Please go back to the process described under "How to Discover Your Limiting Beliefs and Transform Them" in Chapter 5. Focus the exercise specifically on what you believe about your health and about your body's ability to heal. That process will help you shift to a reality of perfect health.

Ariel's Story

Ariel arranged to meet with me on her way back home from a business trip. I was in Chicago over a period of two weeks, and I was holding one or two sessions a day. As with all clients who come to see me, when Ariel walked in I knew our time together would bring miracles—it was only a matter of allowing the process to unfold.

As I was setting up my computer to record the session, Ariel began to relax on the bed. Before she closed her eyes she said, "I know you will heal me." The statement somehow did not seem right to her so she corrected herself: "I will heal myself with your help." I smiled and said, "Very good," and began to guide her into the regression.

Rather than experiencing another life, however, Ariel began describing to me another dimension. She described it this way:

> *Ariel:* It is not time. It is not physical. Everybody has white robes on. There are tons and tons of beings with human appearance. I am at the forefront of them. There are a couple of other . . . it is like I am on a panel, an advisory committee. There

are maybe five of us in the front. Everybody is looking at us for leadership or direction.

It turns out that Ariel's soul was a guide on the spirit side. She was part of a five-member panel that gave advice to other beings. The panel members were able to hear the thoughts of each individual in the group, and they discussed them before suggesting the best solution. Ariel described the process as follows:

> *Ariel:* We are doing 60 different entities at a time. The panel is discussing options and solutions for many different entities at the same time through thought, through feeling, through vibration. I can feel the different intentions and see the life experiences behind the thoughts for many different entities at the same time. The discussions are among the five of us, and the answers are sent back to the individuals and they float away.

In time it became clear that the entities she saw before her were themselves spirit guides, seeking advice for the souls of human beings living on Earth. The area of expertise of this panel was recovery from physical pain. Ariel let me know that there were other panels in the vicinity, each giving advice on a different area of life.

Working on this panel was Ariel's soul's passion. She was on it because she herself had recovered from physical pain during her human incarnations. She loved teaching without expectations. As a soul she felt very drawn to Earth, as if it were her project, her internship. She saw herself as a student. I asked her to go to the moment when her studies began, and she saw herself standing in front of a panel of five guides. Soon she saw these guides merge into one being that presented itself as a man. With that, I began posing the questions Ariel and I had discussed before the regression began.

We spoke about her relationships with her parents and her career, and she was given specific explanations and directions. We also addressed her intimate relationships. But first and foremost, I asked that the pain she was carrying from past relationships—as well as the need to please others and any negative relationship patterns—be released. This was our exchange:

Ariel: He says that I am already working on it, because I have already seen what it looks like now and I know how unattractive it is. He says, "Now choose to release it." I'm telling him, "I choose to release it."

Mira: Feel the intent, because that is really the moment of releasing and letting it go.

Ariel: He is saying, "Very good." Now he is saying, "Embrace the emotion." And I'm saying, "How?" He says, "Instead of running away from it, turn around and embrace it like a bear hug. Imagine it." So I'm going through the layers—possession, jealousy, insecurity. They come from patterns I have seen. It all comes from fear. So I am embracing the fear and I'm saying, "I am not afraid. I love you for what you teach me. And now you can go away."

At the beginning of our session, Ariel had shared that she had a sexually transmitted disease that she wanted to heal. She did not name it, and I didn't ask. The label didn't matter, though, because Spirit knew what needed to be healed. We worked on a few other matters before I asked that we work on healing the body and restoring it to perfect health:

Ariel: He is saying that the blood needs to be cleansed. I am seeing all the veins. They are saying that I need to have a cleansing diet and to not have sex with anyone I have already had sex with.

Mira: I have a feeling this is the clearing of the STD, isn't it?

Ariel: I think so . . . they already released the toxin. He just said, "Any other questions?"

Mira: Please ask him about the healing that just happened—is the STD healed?

Ariel: He says, "Give it a little bit of time, but it's gone."

There were gaps of silence between our exchanges, during which Ariel was observing and feeling the work being done by her guides. My recording indicated that this took a little over four minutes.

Two days after our session, Ariel sent me this e-mail:

> I wanted to tell you a little bit more that I didn't tell you while I was being healed. I mostly just felt energy and tingling on the parts being worked on, and was being told what they were doing. At one point, and this is the only point I saw anyone doing anything, the being was visualized as an extraterrestrial.
>
> Also, the next morning, I was in the shower and I was told to take a bath. I hardly ever take baths. So, I listened, and I dumped the shampoo bottle into the water to make lots of bubbles as I was told. Immediately after I laid down, I went very quickly back to the place where I was when I was with you the previous day. I asked why he had to appear as a man, and he said it was best for me. And then I asked why does he look the same all the time, and he changed into an old Asian-looking man and said, "How's that? That better?" Yes, I'm chuckling. Anyhow, he told me further cleansing needed to take place. He told me when I was done and could rinse off. When I stood up with the bubbles all over me, he said, "Doesn't that tingling feel the same as the energy?" Which, of course, it did. I felt further healing that day and have been told that it will still take a little time.

It was no surprise that Ariel's healing continued after our session. Such is usually the case with my clients. The transformation that is set in motion is all-encompassing. It begins on an emotional and energy level during our time together. During the days that follow, the body's neurological and cellular structures reflect those changes. The healing that was created by Ariel's guides was instantaneous, but because of the nature of physical matter, sometimes a little more time may be needed for the work to be fully experienced in the body.

Approximately two months later, Ariel e-mailed me again. This time, she had good news to report: "I went to the doctor two weeks ago and was tested [for the STD], and just found out today that all tests came back negative—I am cured. Thank you so much for the gift that you gave to me and others!"

This news made me so very happy. I love hearing from my clients after our time together, receiving updates on how their lives have changed. I e-mailed Ariel back and asked her if I could include the story of her healing in this book. Her response was very gracious and informative as to why her body was healed of the STD. She wrote:

> Yes, it would be wonderful if you could share my story in your book. I hope it will help others as well. However, I think mine might be a rather rare case because I believed deeply. But I know with all my heart that anyone can heal their physical body from anything, or better yet, prevent illness from beginning in their body. The body is deeply connected to the mind, and our spirit/soul has the ability to heal both.
>
> I had to follow additional instructions, and I have also been led to read and understand other things that affect our body and healing, such as nutrition, exercise, meditation, forgiveness, and love.
>
> The disease was herpes. It can be medically treated and controlled with prescription drugs, but it is not able to be cured. I got the disease from my ex-husband. I believe what Louise Hay has said, that diseases will show up in your body where unforgiveness lies. For me, the bitterness I was holding against the past men in my life, I believe, helped manifest my body's inability to guard against the disease. I have now forgiven and have thanked all of them in my mind for contributing to me being the person I am right now. I know now that they were all on their own journey and just happened to intersect with mine.

I love how Ariel says that she was healed because she believed. She believed her soul *could* heal her body. She believed our session *could* help her heal. And during our session she told me that she expected and intended to be healed through our work. Ariel humbly said that hers might be a rather rare case, because she believed deeply that she would be healed. In reality, everyone who has experienced a healing did so because he or she believed that the body would transcend the conditions.

There are incarnations where the soul chooses to experience life in a body that is born with defects, or with a mind that does not operate like everyone else's. This choice is made so that the soul can create using the abilities and opportunities that remain unhindered by the condition. These people may not be able to cure the condition in the body, but they have the opportunity to heal emotionally—to change their belief that they are deficient or abnormal. Once we understand why the illness was chosen, and in what ways our soul sought to benefit from the experience, the potential for a very enriching and fulfilling life can be nurtured into fruition.

Recently, I had a past-life regression with a young man who began to develop muscular dystrophy as a toddler. He is paralyzed and needs the constant care of his family. He relived a life where he saw how members of his current family had, each in his or her own way, assisted in his execution on political grounds. In this life, his family was being given the opportunity to balance that past-life experience and take care of him. By choosing an incarnation with such a debilitating condition, his soul is learning what it is like to not have mobility. He's learning how to create a fulfilling life through his creativity, the sharpness of his mind, and the strength of his ability to communicate.

All illnesses begin on an emotional level. Our bodies are not helplessly at the mercy of mysterious viruses or genetic traits. Our bodies are nothing but obliging partners on our journey through life. In Ariel's case, the STD was allowed into her body because it reflected her unresolved emotions toward her former partners. Ariel knew a healing that far exceeded the doctors' prognosis would be possible for her. After our session, she anchored the work by eating differently, exercising, and shifting her thoughts toward forgiveness, gratitude, and love.

I invite you to see any disease as a messenger, pointing toward an emotional issue you have not yet addressed. I am continually amazed by how clever and sometimes very literal our bodies are at manifesting physical representations of emotional challenges. In my sessions, I will ask which unresolved issues are causing physical discomforts. Once the emotional issue is resolved, the cells never fail to reflect the new state of being.

The next time you experience aches or have an accident, ask your body what message it's delivering to you. In moments of meditation, ask for your Higher Self to reveal what you need to let go of and what you need to learn. I have found Louise Hay's book *You Can Heal Your Life* to be a good, quick guide that always points me in the right direction.

When you become aware of the whole picture and how the discomfort serves you, thank your body. Tell your body that the information has been delivered and that it can begin to heal now. Then, have your mind and your spirit work in unison to relieve the emotional imbalance. The physical healing will soon follow.

Exercise: Heal Through Regression

If you have a physical condition you are looking to release, I encourage you to explore the situation through regression. You can use the transcript in Appendix A or use the guided regression on my CD set, *Healing Through Past-Life Regression . . . and Beyond.* You can reach out to me for a personal session, join me for a workshop where I guide participants through regressions, or find a practitioner in your own area. However you proceed, know that you are already aligned with the power offered through this tool for healing.

Set aside at least 40 minutes of quiet time. If you have pets at home, make sure they're out of the room. Before you begin the regression, create the general intention that you are open to exploring a life that will assist in your healing. Ask your Higher Self to lead you to a life that will help you understand your health challenges. Then simply play the recording and trust the process. After you come out of the regression, allow yourself to process the experience in whatever way feels right to you. Journal, take a bath, go for a walk, drink a glass of water, or simply sit quietly, reflecting on your life. Then, bring the insights into your everyday life and trust in your body's ability to heal.

We have discussed how to heal the body of physical symptoms using the knowledge that all possible realities are presently
available for us to choose the reality we desire. Now I would like to
shift our explorations of consciousness to sharing some regression
stories that teach us how loved we are by Source, which will help
us heal our emotions regarding our worth and deservingness.

CHAPTER 9

YOU HAVE
THE RIGHT TO
LOVE YOURSELF

The idea of love—loving yourself and others—was the essential theme of the lifetime that Dr. Wayne Dyer relived during his regression with me. Here I offer only the essence of the story, as the full text of it appears in Wayne's book *Wishes Fulfilled*.

Wayne saw himself living in a desert, a young man whose father had been murdered. He ended up leaving the life of his Arab tribe and working on a boat that brought him to a new land. There he fell in love with a woman, and they soon married. He later took a job on a ship and was excited to travel and discover new territories. As Wayne said during the regression, "There's talk of islands and people who live on them all across the sea. And that excites me. And I go, and I leave her. She's pregnant. But I leave anyway. It just sounds so enticing to find something that no one's ever seen before. It's like a great adventure."

After a long time at sea, the crew discovered an island. The inhabitants were friendly, but the captain and his men were cruel and vicious with them because they were different. As the man he was in that life, Wayne attempted to stop the violence but was unable to. The boat sailed back, and he returned home to the news that his wife has died and no one knew anything about the son she'd given birth to. This made him feel very sad and guilty; as time went on, the sadness stayed with him. He was troubled by all the violence, all the killing, the lack of love, and how people focused on surviving by taking from and hurting one another. He knew there was a different way of living and being, thanks to messages he had received while in a cave.

Wayne described how he saw himself in this cave, in which bright light came through the ceiling. While sitting in the light, he was illuminated by awareness of eternal truths—and they were all about love. One of these truths was, "If you share it, you multiply it. If you hoard it, you lose it."

Wayne felt compelled to share these ideas with people, but he knew they would not hear him. He said, "This truth is just so clear, so clear. You just have to love each other. Love yourself. Love each other." Next, he saw how his long-lost son in that life had come to him, and how he was attempting to share these truths with the boy:

> *Wayne:* I tell him to remember these things. That these are great truths. That when you share, you multiply. When you hoard, you lose. When you do less to other people, you get more. That by being humble and gentle and soft, you get so much more. I'm telling you. You get so close to God. That light is God coming through there. That light is God. It is just so bright. I can see it. Here it comes again. It starts up here, and it goes like this. You just swim in it. You just bathe in this light. It's all so easy. Just tell them that this is easy. It's not hard. It's natural. It's normal. It's what you came from. It's what you are. Find out what you are, and be that. Don't find out what you aren't and try to be that. It's just another truth. One of those simple, simple truths. Be who you are instead of who you're not.
>
> And you can't be anything other than what you are anyway. It is an illusion. If you try to be something that you are not, you can't be anything you're not. You're not hate, you're not killing. That's not who you are. Be who you are. All of that other stuff is not who you are . . . just be who you are.

My son looks perplexed. He thinks I'm a crazy old man. I am a crazy old man. Everyone around me . . . the only one who understood this was, oh my goodness, that beautiful woman. I only knew her for such a short time. And then I left her. She knew this. She waited. She didn't die of something in her chest. She was killed.

My son just told me that. She was killed, too, while I was gone. Everything you love, you lose when you lose the love. Everything you love you lose when you lose the love. So simple. She was murdered, raped. My son wants to know how I feel about the rapist.

"How do you feel, Dad, about the people who killed the woman you love?"

And the light is there. And you can go into it or you can go around it. When you go into it, there's only love, and if I try to go around, it's dark. And it makes me want to kill those motherfuckers.

When I go into the light, I love the rapists. When you lose the love, that's it. When you lose the love, you lose who you are because who you are love. And all the rest of the time you wander around in the darkness just trying to avoid the light, which just calls you, pulls you toward it. It wants to be in it so much. It's too bright. It blinds you with its brightness.

You can really love the people who kill the woman you love. I guess . . . I guess I can because that's who I am. When you love, there's just no room for anything else. If you love, there's just no such thing as nonlove. It's all you have to give away. It's when you leave the spotlight, when you leave the light that's coming into this cave . . . see it come in like this, and then there's all these dark places around it.

And you want me to go into the dark places. But I can't. Because I am the same as that light. That's who I am. And it saddens me, but it seems to me that's what I'm here for.

He tells me that she loved me so much. She waited and waited and waited, and I let her down. Because I had to seek out my adventure. I had to find the new places. And all the while I didn't have to go anywhere.

He says he can't do it. And I say to him, "You're just not ready, but it is who you are, too."

And I got up and walked into that light. I can see it now. And I left him, too . . . bewildered. And I went into that light, and I let myself float into it. I looked down at him, "My son, just move over a few inches into the light. It's just a few inches away. Just slide over, and you'll be in the light. Here is the light and you are here. Just move over here. You just have to move this far."

You know what he said? "Fuck you. You crazy old man. I'm going to get those guys."

As Wayne so poignantly learned, we always have the choice to align ourselves with the Light and be in the vibrational essence of love.

Serena's Story

Following the profound regression I conducted with Wayne, he said to me, "I know someone else who would love to see you." He was thinking of his daughter Serena. I did meet with Serena, and found that her regression reveals how loved and desired we are by All That Is. It teaches us that prior to our existence, there was an imbalance—a void in All That Is that could only be filled by a specific energy. Our souls were each created to embody that one particular energy. From the moment the need for each of us was perceived, even before our souls were born, we have been wanted, treasured, and loved.

Once her regression began, Serena described a place with sand and pyramids. It was a portal between dimensions. Everybody who came to Earth—newly created souls, already existing souls, and spirit guides—had to come through this plane first. Everything that was to be developed on Earth was already known in this dimension, and was depicted as images on the inside walls of the pyramids. I asked Serena to describe the place in more detail. She said:

> *Serena:* It's this big sandy desert that is very peaceful. There's no air. There's no wind. It's like Earth but not really. It's above

Earth. It's not really above it because Earth is not below it. It's just another space. . . . I'm a shepherd here. Not of animals but of people. I guide them. That's why I'm important. I'm someone who guides them.

Mira: Do you guide the new souls only? Or do you guide the other beings who enter?

Serena: I guide everybody.

Mira: Describe how that looks and feels to you.

Serena: It feels really loving. There's no judgment toward any of the new beings because they come perfect. They come peacefully. They don't have a bad cell in them. It feels very much like an honor. Even the people I see who will cause pain or something down the line, it's all okay to me. I really love them all.

Mira: How do you see this information? Is it something you receive? Or is it something you look at the wall and see?

Serena: It's a feeling that I get. I can see their soul. I just know that they have within them a path they're on . . . that some of them will cause hurt and pain. It's okay because they're still perfect even though they're going to do that. They're more brave. They chose that. And it's not easy.

Mira: It's not easy to cause hurt and pain?

Serena: They're very important people.

Mira: Please tell me.

Serena: Everybody who comes to Earth comes through here first. . . . Everybody has a combination of all these colors that make up their soul. Everybody's combination is a little bit different. Some of these people have a little bit more dark. It doesn't mean that they're bad. It just means that there has to be light and dark. It has to be a balance. For the people who have more dark, it's almost like navy because it's not quite black. I really love them. They signed on to take on a lot. God created them to be teachers, but they don't know that they're teachers. Teachers' energy is more yellow. They're not teachers like Jesus is a teacher who teaches the planet. They're teachers who teach out of their actions. You kind of learn from them not to be that energy. It's important for everyone to love them. The reason I do this job is because God knows that I do love them. For me, I cannot judge them just because they have darker colors.

Mira: How does a soul go into a physical being's body?

Serena: That doesn't happen here. It's the plane before Earth. But there's another plane.

Mira: How does that transition from your plane to the Earth plane happen?

Serena: It happens slowly. It feels like my plane is where you can just be. Your soul can be filled again with colors and energies it needs for its journey. In the next plane your assignment becomes more clear. In mine you just have energies. In the next plane it becomes clearer what your sole purpose will be. There's a lot more planes you go through.

But your colors can change in your life while you are incarnated. Your colors can change because you can choose to change them.

The plane Serena was seeing was a place souls pass through on their way to being incarnated. On that plane souls get their colors, and the different color combinations give each soul its uniqueness.

One of the portals through which souls arrived on her plane was specifically for newly created souls, and I asked if she could go through that portal to see how new souls are created. The description she gave reminds me of the description Albert gave of what the God energy is like—a very subtle but very powerful milky-white brightness:

Serena: When you go into the white portal, you go, instead of going down in my plane, you go up. You're at the beginning of everything.

Mira: What's around you?

Serena: White. Everything is white. It doesn't feel empty. It is the source of everything. Everything is there. Everything you want is there, but it's not there.

Every time a new soul is created, which is not that common anymore because the Earth is more complete . . . when new souls are created, it's because there's a need for that. There's a need for a new type of energy that hasn't been created before. That's the only reason a new soul is created. Those new souls are like little eggs, very fragile. Everything is very new to them. The whole experience is very new for them. So when they go through all these planes and then to Earth, nothing is familiar. Nothing is a memory. So for these new souls, sometimes they have to come in gently. Everything can be very big for them and overwhelming.

Mira: How is the need for a new soul known?

Serena: Because there becomes a gap in an energy system that cannot be balanced with the guides, and they know this. It's like God knows this. It's like the collective energy knows. It's like your body. Your body is your own world. Everything works together to stay balanced. But sometimes you have a craving for something like salt. You don't know why, but the rest of you does. It needs it for something. The new soul that comes in is needed for something. I don't really know what because I'm not the creator.

Mira: This place where these new souls are created . . . is this the only place for the Earth and all other dimensions, or do all dimensions have their own places for creation?

Serena: All dimensions have their own places of creation. And there are so many dimensions. Sometimes the dimensions merge and there's even more places of creation. Just so many different beings out there that we don't even know of yet. God knows, but we don't as people.

Mira: What is the composition of these new souls? How do they get made? Can you see the process and describe it for me?

Serena: They don't have a physical form yet. I don't know when they do . . . that's down the line. It's just this white place. It's this energy that is just floating. It's like cells that start to come together because there's a magnetic pull way down below for this energy. The Earth already knows what it needs. It's sort of sending out an intention to have it created. It's created. All the right energies need to come together. And then this whiteness that's blank goes through this white portal and comes to where I usually am, which is where souls get colors. The colors will make up more of its composition. And then it goes and gets a purpose created for it. All of this is already established by the thing that needed it. So then it goes down a line, and then it's born.

I was truly amazed by this revelation. After the session with Serena, it felt as if I had been gently awakened. It was as if the spark of divinity had been reignited in me, reminding me of my true nature. It started as this whisper in the quiet of my mind: "All That Is felt a void that could only be complete by *my* unique presence. I am no coincidence. I am desired. God created me because the One considers me an important part of the Universe."

Tears of awe filled up my eyes as I felt how loved I am by Source. The powerful energy of this light of love was not to be denied. It took a hold of me. The spark of this understanding grew bigger and bigger with the passing of each day. Over time, it has gently shifted the way I see myself and my worth as a person.

The Soul's Purpose

Ariel, whose story of healing I shared in the previous chapter, also experienced the powerful knowing that her being was brought about by Spirit seeking to create and experience through her.

When Ariel stood in front of her panel of five guides, she recognized that their presence had a great significance for her. She described this awareness as follows:

Ariel: They are more than a teacher. They are almost like a parent. They are more enlightened. I trust them. I have love for them, and they have love for me. But I don't know where they are from. It just is. I am trying to find out how they were assigned to me.

Mira: Just ask them. They will tell you.

Ariel: They created me. I am almost like their child. They manifested me. I said, "Why?" They said, "'Cause we felt like it."

Mira: Why are souls being created?

Ariel: They said that there is infinite space to fill up and it will never be filled up. Oh . . . ! Oh! I thought souls were all created at the same time. No. They are saying that souls are still being created. They say I am stuck on time.

Mira: Ask them to explain.

Ariel: Time is an illusion of course, but . . . time was created by spirit entities participating in physical reality for the purpose of restraint, limit. Physical reality has to learn to not have limits. I am a piece of something. All of me is not this. I am a piece of them.

Mira: Ask them to explain about you being a piece of them.

Ariel: They manifested me to learn compassion.

Your soul is created to fulfill a purpose. This idea, shared by both Serena and Ariel, has the power to take our oldest negative conditioning and turn it into dust. Yet most of us were never taught that our existence was asked for by God. And that, because God asked for us, *we deserve to be*. Most of us are raised to believe that we need to prove our worth and that we must take certain steps to deserve the grace of God. Our very existence is the proof of how worthy we are to the Universe. We wouldn't exist if we were not desired and unconditionally loved, even before we were created.

The story below is an example of how this limiting assumption can fall away as soon as we discover that we are already loved by Source.

I was sitting on the beach, waiting for the sun to set. As I was taking in the natural beauty that surrounded me, I noticed a young man nearby with a camera. He was taking picture after picture of the rainbow that was dancing in the sky. I could tell we shared a certain awe in the face of nature's beauty, so I decided to strike up a conversation. Very quickly, we dove into deep and meaningful subjects.

Sam shared with me that he was at a crossroads. He felt that his old life was over, and yet he had not decided on a new path. A few days before, he'd written down three goals he had for himself. Even though we'd just met, he said he felt comfortable sharing them with me.

His first goal was to own a home. As I heard this, I nodded with understanding—it was a valid desire.

His second goal was to "do something great/important. Truly achieve greatness and be able to recognize that quality in myself." I nodded again. What an admirable goal! Each of us knows that there is something great inside of us; we feel it deep within. It nags at us in the still, quiet moments of our day, reminding us of a promise we made to ourselves long ago.

This sense is our own essence trying to express itself. It is the might of Source reflected in us; it is the inextinguishable flame that is looking to grow and fully express into the world. It's our greatness. It has every one of us seek out our purpose, and keeps us restless until we express our unique gifts in meaningful and fulfilling ways—ways that allow for the God inside of us to expand and truly know itself as greatness.

So far, I was fully in support of Sam's goals. That was, until we got to number three. Sam's third goal was to "earn the privilege to deserve respect from anyone and everyone." This time I cringed.

We don't need to earn anything in order to deserve. We *already* deserve everything. But I am aware that without context, these words would be meaningless. So I decided to tell Sam what Serena's regression had taught me.

I described her session in as much detail as possible. As I finished the story, Sam looked in my eyes and said, "Oh, wow!" He continued to look at me, but I could tell he no longer saw me. I knew he was moved. I could see the layers of belief powerfully shifting, like the Earth's tectonic plates, forming a new topography in his mind.

By this time the sun was setting, and the majestic beauty of the red and orange hues engulfed us both. In the silence of the moment we both reconnected to the truth of who we are and how much we deserve.

Several months later, I reached out to Sam. I told him about the book I was writing and asked if I could include the story of our conversation. He graciously agreed. He sent me a text message with his original goals. He also added a comment.

"Goals 2 and 3 are kinda the same," he wrote. "But I remember you convincing me of the truth that everyone already deserves respect, just for being here on Earth."

A sense of exaltation moved through my body. He heard me! And not only did he hear me, but he also *believed* me.

Giving full expression to our greatness is our God-given right. Each of us already has the full love, support, and admiration of All That Is on the path of our expansion. It is only our belief that we need to "earn" the privilege to deserve that keeps us from fully knowing and expressing the greatness of who we already are.

Who Expelled Whom?

Divine power is eternally present in us. It is the seed that is planted at our core in the moment of our creation. Yet once we are born on Earth, we forget about our Divine nature, just as Sam did. We trust only our five senses, and we feel alone and removed from

Source. We feel we need to work hard to prove ourselves, so we can deserve the grace of God. We seek to reconnect to the feeling of bliss our soul remembers, to overcome the feeling of separateness. That perception of separateness—the belief that our goal is outside of us—has long been represented by the story of Adam and Eve being expelled from the Garden of Eden.

Kabbalah is the Judaic study of the great mysteries of the Divine. Kabbalah's fundamental text is the Sefer ha-Zohar, commonly called the Zohar, which means "the Book of Radiance" or "the Book of Splendor." The Zohar is an account of the adventures of rabbis wandering through the hills of Galilee, intermixed with teachings, through their conversations, on the hidden meaning of the Torah.

In a radically different interpretation of the Garden of Eden story, the Zohar suggests that instead of God expelling Adam from the Garden, Adam actually expelled God—by divorcing himself from God's Divine feminine form, the Shekinah.

Kabbalah teaches us that God is equally male and female, yet it is up to human beings to make God whole by manifesting a reality of God on Earth that honors both its masculine and feminine aspects. According to Kabbalah, Adam's sin was that he sought only the physical bonding with Shekinah. In doing so, he separated Shekinah from the other nine emanations, or *sephirot*, of Spirit and disrupted the unity of the Universe. As a result, Adam expelled God from the Garden of Eden.

As Kabbalah scholar Daniel Matt explains in an interview for the *San Francisco Chronicle,* "I think what the Zohar means is that we're still in the garden but we just don't realize it because we've lost touch with the spiritual dimension of life. The challenge then comes to reestablish our relationship with God, to rediscover some intimacy with the spiritual dimension of life."

The Zohar teaches us that we continue to reside in the Garden of Eden, even now. Unfortunately, we don't recognize it because we have separated ourselves from God. In order to experience ourselves as living in the paradise of Divine love, we need to reconnect—to reestablish our relationship with the Infinite. To feel the presence of Source, we don't need to seek something outside of ourselves. Source experienced the need for us and created us. By tuning within and appreciating ourselves as a magnificent creation of God, containing both its masculine and feminine aspects, we reaffirm our origin. By appreciating the beauty of what God has created in us, we are appreciating our Source. Because in truth, we *are* what we came from. We are God. In knowing our Divine radiance, we know God.

Damian's Story

Damian was lying on the couch in my office, in a deep trance state. He had just relived a life that had brought out many emotions. I asked him to drift away from those scenes and allow images of the next lifetime to emerge. What he began describing surprised me:

Damian: It's a flower. Orangish; bloomed with a very green and very thin stem. Almost don't know how the flower is being held up from such a small stem. And it's me. And it's breathing. It almost expands and contracts.

Mira: Did you say the flower is you?

Damian: Yes.

Mira: How does it feel to be the flower?

Damian: It feels amazing. I open and I close. I am in complete control of when I open and close. Ha! And I am expansive! And I am interesting. I am detailed. I am in a garden.

Mira: Tell me about your surroundings.

Damian: Nobody is like me. Nobody. There's a few other small flowers, but I am the most free, the most expressive . . . I feel this confidence comes from being in this flower. I have a very expansive, impressive top. But such a thin stem! And this stem somehow holds me up. I can never leave and never move from there, and that is just okay.

Mira: Do you ever wonder what it would be like to be able to move and leave?

Damian: I don't even care. Why would I want to leave this? I have everything I need. I like that I have this essence, this energy, and this powerful beauty, and that [the other flowers] see it.

Mira: How did you come to be this flower, this beautiful flower with such a beautiful, powerful essence?

Damian: I don't remember. I don't remember the process to get there. Almost like I was already there. So I don't even know if I grew.

Mira: It feels like you were always there?

Damian: Yeah. You know, that is exactly it. It feels eternal.

Mira: How do you feel about the sun?

Damian: That's what I worship. I feel that the sun has made me this beautiful. Because when I see the sun I open up. Almost like the sun is calling me to open up. And then I leave.

Mira: What do you mean by that?

Damian: I go up toward the sun and I am leaving the flower. Whatever I am has left that flower. And I don't know why and I want to go back. But I don't think that is the plan. That was amazing! Now I know . . . wow! Now I am having the realization that I wasn't that flower. But I was that flower, too.

Mira: Tell me more about this realization.

Damian: I'm spiraling upward. It's like I had reached a point of ecstasy beyond the flower and that was necessary. And now I spiral up toward the sun. And I see I'm leaving the flower. And that is when I realize I wasn't the flower. I mean, I was the flower, but I wasn't the flower.

As Damian was drifting up, he understood that he was also Spirit knowing itself as the flower. There was no separation between the soul and its expression in the physical. The soul that created the flower marveled at its creation, and the flower—as the physical representation—saw its own beauty in the energy of its Source. The flower shows us how natural it is to recognize what is good and praiseworthy about us. The flower lived as Rumi teaches us: "Shine like the whole universe is yours!"

In that moment of loving and fully expressing its beauty, the flower was fulfilling the purpose of its existence. The flower did not doubt whether it deserved to be so beautiful or whether it was allowed to enjoy its perfection. The flower simply enjoyed what it was and fully gave it expression.

Allow yourself to be like the flower. Say out loud to yourself, "I deserve to exist. I am beautiful and I love myself." How does saying those words make you feel? If it causes any disbelief or discomfort, I encourage you to shake off all your uneasy feelings. Look to your Divine essence and treasure it, for it is God's light residing in you. Practice what the Bible teaches us: "Finally, brothers and sisters, whatever is true, whatever is noble, whatever is right, whatever is pure, whatever is lovely, whatever is admirable—if anything is excellent or praiseworthy—think about such things" (Philippians 4:8).

Think about the great qualities and attributes you have. Act in ways that reflect your magnificence. Speak lovingly of the beautiful person you are. Fall in love with yourself. Nurture yourself gently as a gardener who is growing a unique rose. Remind yourself that Source treasures you for the person you find yourself to be today. Your unique combination of energies is no coincidence; it was asked for. You belong in this world. You belong in the ever-expansive energy of God. You are an important and valued part of All That Is.

You deserve to exist. You deserve the unconditional love that Source has for you. All That Is experienced a deep need that only your soul could satisfy. Take this to heart and fill yourself with the paradigm-shattering power of the love that created you.

The realization that each one of us was asked for by all of existence, by God, has profound implications. This seed of truth carries enormous power. It holds the potential to awaken each and every one of us from the slumber of denial and the forgetfulness of our essence. If I were to write the code future generations would live by, the very first sentences would read as follows:

> Rejoice in your existence, dear one. All That Is created you because it desires to know itself through the unique combination of energies that you are, and the unique perspective that you provide. You already deserve. You are unconditionally loved and enormously valued for who you are. You are supported in every step of your glorious expansion. Love yourself as God loves you. Now go and live your life, treasuring yourself the way Source treasures you, fully expressing your Divine beauty, and forever knowing the truth of who you are.

Exercise: Love Yourself Daily

I encourage you to create a daily practice of connecting with Source and with your own Divine nature. Set aside 20 minutes of uninterrupted time, either at the beginning or at the end of the day. Make it your time to open up to loving and trusting yourself. Become aware of your breath. As you slow your breath down, begin by saying the word *love* in your mind. Feel the energy of love arise within you as you evoke it with this chant. Trust your intuition, and the moment it feels right, begin saying in your mind, *I am love.* And when it feels right again change that to *I love myself.* Feel the energy of love moving through your body. Let it embrace you. Let it assure you how loved and supported you are. Remember, there is no goal to this meditation other than to soothe yourself and feel the warm energy of God's love for you—and your own love for yourself. When you come out of the meditation, allow the peaceful and nurturing energy of love to flow into your daily life.

For those of you who prefer to meditate with a guided recording, I offer a meditation that I have created and listen to every day. It is focused around the ideas of self-love and trust. Please download this recording for free from my website: www.mirakelley.com/meditation -download.

It will be my greatest joy to support you in the affirmation of your worth and deservingness through this meditation. It will aid you in awakening to your beautiful essence, embracing the unconditional love that Source has for you, and recognizing that you truly deserve to express yourself to the fullest.

If you were to retain any of the many ideas shared in this book, I hope it is the knowingness that you deserve, that you are supported and unconditionally loved by Source. When allowed in, this profound understanding will transform your life as it has mine. It has allowed me to fully dive into the uniqueness of who I am, and to express it so that I can create a life of meaning and satisfaction. In the chapter that follows, I will share with you how my life changed once I began to recognize and trust that the light of God itself shined through me.

CHAPTER 10

TRUST YOURSELF AND FOLLOW YOUR EXCITEMENT

As an individualized entity, a soul is free to create experiences in order to grow in its awareness. By doing so it fulfills its purpose, which is to grow and learn more about itself. Through that, your soul helps All That Is know more about *itself.*

When a soul prepares for a physical incarnation, the plan it creates is usually very general. Sometimes specific details may be added, but for the most part the soul simply picks a theme or two that it is looking to explore. These themes are more like broad strokes of intent, rather than step-by-step scripts. They are chosen to benefit the Oversoul, all other soul counterparts, the soul's family group, and ultimately, All That Is.

We could say that one's theme is one's destiny. However, that is where any notion of predetermination ends. The real force in operation once we incarnate is free will—the ability to choose. What seems like destiny to a person is a theme that was freely chosen by its soul. Once a theme is selected for an incarnation, that person is free to explore the theme in any way he or she chooses. Take, for example, the theme of abundance. The soul may choose to be born into a poor, middle-class, or rich family.

From there, the person is free to choose how to experience his relationship with money. Think of all the self-made millionaires, all those heirs who have wasted fortunes, and the countless people who struggle from paycheck to paycheck. Another example is the theme of love. Your soul would learn equally valid lessons about love by your being a very jealous and possessive person in your intimate relationships as it would by your creating harmonious, loving partnerships based on mutual respect and appreciation.

The theme of John's present life is *understanding,* but his Higher Self told me that it was not preordained how John would explore this theme. I was told that he was doing well so far, but he may eventually choose to become physically ill in order to learn about understanding. In other words, choices and adjustments are constantly being made during the progress of a life. In a part of my conversation with the Higher Self, I was told that John has other soul counterparts who have explored the themes of life and death, often through dying in war.

Because balanced understanding is the Oversoul's approach, several soul fragments will explore the same theme, each in its own way. This is where the concept of karma fits in. Karma, as discussed further below, is simply the Oversoul's desire to know the same theme through different points of view. Therefore, one who has murdered in one life may have a counterpart in a different life who counsels murderers, prevents a murder from happening, becomes the victim himself, or is born as the parent of the counterpart's victim. In each case, the soul has the chance to explore resolving conflicts through love. The variations are limitless, and the soul is free to choose how to uniquely know itself through that theme.

The True Meaning of Karma

Karma is a representation of the soul's desire for balance in its experiences. It represents the soul's quest to learn from different perspectives. Every soul grows in understanding by experiencing existence from different points of view. These different perspectives could be lived through one life, with a person going from poor to rich, for example. Or it could happen over many lifetimes, such as a person experiencing the theme of abundance in its different variations.

There is no judgment in karma; it is not punitive. It is not imposed upon you from the outside—it's simply the Oversoul's desire for balance in its learning. If your soul feels the need to balance its energies based on prior experiences—whether in the same life or in another—you will find the most appropriate way to achieve that balance. The result is what we call karma. Every action creates an outcome. When you experience the resulting effect, you can evaluate it and decide whether that's the outcome you prefer. If so, you have learned about a preference you have. If, on the other hand, the effect is displeasing to you, you simply need to make the choice to act differently the next time.

Sadly, we have applied a sense of judgment to the term *karma*. This gives us yet another way to play small, to play the victim. It is ironic, because you alone have the power to free yourself from the effects of karma. The commonly held concept of karma as payback for old debts is false. Balancing the negative energies and experiences you've created does not mean that you need to experience negativity. You can choose to have a conscious recognition of your desire to balance your life, and you can then take positive actions that will allow you to balance the situation as it is. Know that you are free to choose who you are. With every choice, you are directing your experience. You are growing and expanding with every step you take, in the direction you prefer. You are free to be who you want to be, and to experience life as that person.

We ourselves are the only ones who are judging how well we do in our incarnations. There is no one "up there" keeping score. We live to our own satisfaction. We take on a life because we are eager to be more, to experience more, and to create more. It is our joy to be of service through the very existence of our lives.

The Purpose of Themes

Once we become aware of our themes, we are free to either continue working within that lesson's parameters or to bring them to conclusion. Even though the themes are chosen before we are born, we can complete them midlife, and then the soul will choose a new theme to be explored. It's possible to bring a theme to conclusion rather than working through it for the rest of our lives. We have chosen to be born at a time when the expansion of the collective consciousness is being explored as a shared theme. Therefore, our individual themes operate within the collective theme—consciousness shift—that we have all agreed upon.

I invite you to place this new idea at the back of your mind. Next time your all-familiar challenge in life presents itself, remind yourself that your lesson comes with a built-in detonation button. All you have to do is explore different approaches to living that theme. When you find the mental attitude that makes you feel in harmony with all of life, even while your theme still lurks in the corners of your mind, you can be certain that you are sitting directly on top of that button. The moment you choose to (and I assure you that the moment inevitably comes once you are ready), you will put an end to the old theme. A sense of completion and clear understanding will follow. But no matter how enjoyable the view from the peak you have conquered, the explorer in you will dream of new vistas. That is when you will pick yourself a new theme on a soul level through which to explore creation. And life will seamlessly continue.

Exercise: Identify Your Themes

To do this process, set aside 15 to 20 minutes of quiet time. Have your journal or a piece of paper you can write on nearby. Take a deep breath and release it slowly. Now think about the recurring patterns in your life. In what areas are you having repeated challenges? Some of the common lessons we explore have to do with abundance, relationships, and power. Do any of those resonate with you? When you contemplate following your dreams, what fears arise for you? When you're doing what you love—what's easy for you, what you are particularly good at—what obstacles get in your way? Write down everything that comes up.

An example from my life was my fear of public speaking. It excited me to share what I was learning with others, yet part of me was afraid to be seen by people. I had to overcome this fear and release the theme of powerlessness as part of becoming who I am today.

When you are done writing everything you can think of to answer the questions above, read all your answers and look for the common thread. Look for the essence at the core of all your answers. That is your theme.

In the moments and days that follow, I recommend that you work through the process called "How to Discover Your Limiting Beliefs and Transform Them" from Chapter 5. At its core, your theme is a neutral idea—it is simply a field of study for your soul. It is the beliefs you have attached to it that have turned it into a challenge. By replacing the negative beliefs with supportive assumptions, you will be able to redefine your theme and have it become a positive experience—and eventually, to release it altogether.

The discussion of themes is an appropriate place for me to address the idea of mistakes. No matter how hard it is for us to forgive ourselves, it's important to understand that there are no failures in life. Every point of view provides learning and growth. Every experience is beneficial for our soul's expansion. Therefore, it's all good. It really is.

You may not prefer certain situations in your life, but that doesn't mean you need to think of them in negative terms. Do not devalue yourself or your experiences. Everything you create is valuable to your soul. Everything is appreciated and cherished. Know that the experiences you no longer prefer have served you, even if they only taught you that a particular way is not how you want to know yourself.

You cannot change what you're fighting against. Change comes when you love, accept, and appreciate the totality of yourself. No war—internal or external—has ever brought permanent peace. Only love and forgiveness can bring peace. You no longer need to be involved in battling with yourself. Make peace with yourself by unconditionally embracing the goodness that you are. Bring the situations that make you feel shame into your heart. Neutralize the negative charge by infusing them with your love. Forgive yourself and love yourself for what you have learned. If you do this, you will be able to effortlessly transcend what you fought before. You will be able to transform any situation. You will be able to mold your life in the direction of your dreams, even while continuing to explore your themes.

Embrace the Power Within

It is only possible to shift out of a situation once you consciously recognize that you are creating your own experience of life. You are not a victim of anything or anyone; you are a powerful creator. Our culture teaches us that things will always be unfair due to that mysterious occurrence called our "lot in life." But we must recognize that the cultural norm does not need to be our experience. We create our own experience and our own reality.

Up to this point, your life experience may have been based on the beliefs of those around you, beliefs you have unconsciously absorbed or taken for granted. But those are just thoughts playing in your mind like a scratched record that plays the same tune over and over.

From a neurological perspective, the thoughts you have about yourself and your life are nothing more than electrical pulses traveling along cellular pathways in your brain. These pulses and pathways have been created by your body to transfer and assimilate information. Because you have been thinking the same thoughts over and over, these biological structures are very well established. For most of us, they have become the default way to think about particular subjects. That is why it may seem that a more positive thought does not seem true at first: because it contradicts your established neural system. Despite that feeling, stay with the more positive thoughts. Every new thought changes your brain by wiring it differently. Every new thought changes your perspective. Every new thought creates a new reality. Every new thought allows you to become more the person you desire to be.

You have skillfully designed every aspect your life. Now that you are aware of your themes, you are free to choose to try something else. The world does not need to change in order for you to begin feeling better about your life. Instead, focus on transforming your inner world. Trust that, in time, the outside will reflect the changes happening within you.

Become aware of your beliefs. Begin examining them and allowing for new and more supportive thoughts to replace the old ones. You have that power in you. You have the power to change. You are the master of your universe. There is such a profound sense of empowerment and a feeling of belonging when this point of view becomes your outlook on life.

Most of us create "by default"; we don't know we're creating, so we are not able to make conscious choices about what we create. Even "default" creation is a valuable experience. It teaches us that there is something else we would prefer. We are free in this moment to claim, choose, and become—in our thoughts, deeds, and actions—the people we want to be.

Again, true power exists in the present moment, where we create who we choose to be as well as our past and future. It is only in the present moment that we can experience life. As we have explored in this book, the consecutive evolution of events that we think of as "time" is but an illusion—a convenient construct. Our thinking mind, our ego, which is so intensely focused on physical existence, uses it as an organizing tool.

Memories are also created in the present moment. Memories are nothing but thoughts you are thinking in the now. The memories you choose to experience and the way you choose to experience those "prior" events are determined by the present perceptions you hold in your mind and the current beliefs you have about who you are. The things around you—relationships, objects, events—are nothing but neutral occurrences. Nothing in life has an assigned value. It is your interpretation, which is based on your beliefs, that gives circumstances meaning.

You are the one with the power to assign your own subjective values to things based on your unique thinking. For example, a photo of a steak will make some of us salivate and crave a delicious piece of meat. Others, perhaps those of us who believe in veganism, will find the photo repulsive; it will represent everything we stand against. The values of the observer give the same photo the label "good" or "bad."

Similarly, the circumstances in your life are neutral events. It is you who has supplied the "good" and the "bad" labels. Ask yourself, "How did it benefit me to experience these certain negative events in my life?" Every situation is an opportunity to learn—even if the lesson is that you don't want to learn about yourself in that way again! Knowing that every situation is neutral, you can make an intentional decision to note the benefits you have derived from every experience, and then decide the new way in which you are choosing to tell your story. Emphasize the benefits you have experienced and the upsides you gained. By taking this approach—interpreting everything as a positive—you will no longer feel marginalized and self-pitying. After all, no winner is a victim.

You are the storyteller of your life. How would you like your story to be told?

Exercise: How to Break the Bonds of Prior Limitations

I would like to introduce a powerful process that allows for rapid transformation. It will assist you in easily breaking the bonds of prior limitations. This exercise is very helpful, not only for those who are in a challenging place but also for those who are seeking to transform their beliefs about any aspect of life—including self-worth, money, or relationships. You can do this exercise with a therapist or with a trusted friend. You can read the text into a recorder so that you can play it back for yourself. Or you can simply read through the instructions and guide yourself through the process while in a meditative state. Allow your intuition to determine the best way for you to do this exercise, and use your imagination freely. Be sure to give yourself at least 20 minutes of uninterrupted time to complete it.

Assume a comfortable position and close your eyes. After taking a few slow, deep, relaxing breaths, imagine that you're a little baby in your mother's womb. See yourself as the perfect creation that you are. Feel how warm and safe it is to be in your mother's belly. Feel your Divine essence and know that you are nurtured, loved, and always provided for. You have everything you need. Then, allow your imagination to take you through your birth, the way you desire for your birth to have been. Feel what it would be like to take your first breath of air. Imagine what it would feel like to be welcomed into this world with great anticipation, love, and excitement.

Use your imagination to see what it would be like to have the childhood you would like to have had. Be the child who becomes the adult you would like to be now. Do not censor your imagination with restraints about what it was really like, or any other limitations. Paint everything in your head in the best possible light.

How would your parents treat you? Would you like for any events to have unfolded differently? Are there events that would have needed to take place, or those that never would have happened? What truths would your parents and teachers impart to you? Would you like for your family to have more or less money, or to live in different places? Where would you go to school? Would you like to have different friends?

Imagine how this new child, this new you, would be taught about your value and self-worth. What kind of beliefs would you like this child to have about love, relationships, money, work, and everything else? Give the child these new ideas and ways of being. This child trusts you and absorbs what you're teaching as the absolute truth. Feel how these new ways of knowing yourself are permanently imprinted in the energetic and cellular structures of this beautiful child.

See this child grow up and become an adult. See this adult as the ideal version of you. Who do you grow up to be? What is your most fulfilled, most happy life like? What is different about this version of you? How does this version live life?

Next, imagine that the ideal version of you and who you are today are drawn toward one another. Feel the ideal you merging into the current you—feel the two becoming one. Feel as you would feel as this new, ideal you. Feel your vibration rise. Revel in this energy, knowing that this is who you now are. This is a new reality and this is the new you. Commit to living as the new version of yourself.

Within yourself, you contain this child. You've shifted to a reality where you had this child's past. Know that you have now restructured the idea of your childhood. You are now free to speak and act as the adult version of that child. Know that there is nothing from your past to hold you back. Choose your preferred past. The past is created in the present. You create a new present—you create the life of the ideal you—by creating a new past. Choose a past that will support your ideal present, one where you are living your dreams.

By doing this exercise you will enter an altered brain-wave state, a state of hypnosis. Just like my clients, you will come out of this trance state feeling different, as though you are a different person. You will feel lighter. You will feel more optimistic, as if there were less weight on your shoulders and more room to breathe. Through this process you will give yourself permission to become your greatest potential— the true you, the most creative, expressive, and joyful you. Stay with this feeling. Allow it to be encoded in every cell of your body as your new vibration. Trust it, act on it, and from this energy place build upon it the life you would like to have.

If the thought, *But it isn't real!* pops into your head, remember all that you have learned in this book about your possible selves and other parallel realities. Remind yourself that you are the storyteller of your life, and "real" is a very subjective experience. There are many different versions of every possible reality, and each is "real" to those experiencing it. I'm not encouraging you to weave a web of lies to tell your friends; I *am* encouraging you to change your energy, your alignment, your attitudes, and your beliefs. I'm encouraging you to free yourself and experience your life in the way that pleases you. Just because something didn't occur in the life you know and remember does not mean that you cannot derive value from it. You need only experience yourself in a different way. You can switch to a parallel reality where you *are* that person. The only permission you need to live a fulfilling life is your own. Give yourself that permission. Change is that easy.

Miracle After Miracle . . .

I would now like to return to the story I used to open this book—the story of how I switched from being a corporate lawyer to serving people in their spiritual growth and expansion. It is a story of how I broke the bonds of prior limitations and learned that I have wings and I can fly. The continuation of my story is the best possible example I can give you on the biggest lesson I have learned: to trust myself and to follow my excitement to the best of my ability in every moment.

After I experienced a miraculous healing of my TMJ condition through past-life regression, I renewed my excitement for regression. I read every book on past lives and near-death experiences that I could find. In my effort to convey to people how powerful this work is, I gave away as gifts countless copies of what had started it all for me, *Through Time Into Healing* by Brian Weiss. My passion was igniting sparks in many hearts. Despite my demanding work schedule, I went to every past-life seminar I could. I regressed every family member and, most of all, my beloved partner. I even taught my partner how to regress me, and often asked him to do so. As I mentioned earlier in the book, John was the first stranger I had a session with. The positive experience we created together gave me the confidence and desire to put myself out there even more, opening up to seeing clients whenever I could.

Simultaneously, I was working on releasing my limiting beliefs about money. I recognized the fears, as they were always right there staring at me. In my mind it did not seem possible for healers to earn a living. What had brought me to—and kept me in—the legal profession had been my parents' beliefs about money. Using what I was learning through regression, I started to see that my parents themselves had picked up their beliefs from their own families and culture. Once I began unraveling the beliefs, I realized they were assumptions that did not even belong to me. I allowed all the thoughts and fears to arise. I neutralized the emotional charges by meditating, using Emotional Freedom Techniques (EFT, also known as "tapping"), and following the exercises offered in this book. Then I redefined each emotion in the way I chose. I knew that I was my own person, and I had the right to choose how I wanted to see the world and my life. Once my energy around money was clarified, it was as if a whole new world of possibilities opened up for me.

More and more, I allowed myself to become the person I knew myself to be. Because I trusted in regression and put myself out there as much as I could, more and more opportunities began presenting themselves to me.

One of those opportunities was an invitation that came from Brian Weiss himself. Brian and his daughter, Amy, were writing a new book detailing stories people had as a result of attending his workshops, reading his books, listening to his audios, or using regression with their own clients. All of Brian's former students received an e-mail inviting us to contribute to the book. I submitted three stories—two of my own regressions, and one from a client. Even though Brian and Amy received hundreds of stories of regression experiences, all three of mine were selected and were soon published in the book *Miracles Happen*. I am truly grateful to Brian and Amy for the recognition, and for the opportunity to share the lessons my client and I learned.

And then there was a moment when I realized I had expanded so much that I could no longer attempt to fit myself into my old ways of being. It came after I conducted a session for Dr. Wayne Dyer.

Several months before, I had spoken with a friend who told me that Wayne was leading a group of people on a tour through Europe, called "Experiencing the Miraculous." My intuition reverberated at the word *miraculous*. I knew that Wayne had leukemia, and I somehow knew deep down that he was ready for a miracle —the miracle of healing. I shared this intuition with my friend, who was aware that the regression sessions I facilitate have a very powerful healing component. I told her I thought that Wayne may benefit if we worked together, and she encouraged me to reach out and offer a regression session to him.

I could have easily dismissed the suggestion. In fact, initially I did. I had no idea of how to contact Wayne to begin with, and I didn't know whether he would be interested in working with me. I imagined that he had many skilled healers around him. However, the feeling that I needed to speak with him persisted and became more compelling over time. Eventually, I got over my own resistance by reminding myself that I love being of service to others. I told myself that if I am meant to be a tool in the hands of God, then I must allow for the unfolding of whatever miracles need to take place. Several days later, after quite a bit of research, I found Wayne's address and wrote him a letter.

When Wayne called me about a month later, I had forgotten all about the letter. We spoke briefly of the possibility of doing a regression and were about to hang up when I interrupted Wayne's good-bye. Before I knew what I was saying, I heard myself telling him that there was a story of a woman's near-death experience (NDE) I wanted to send him.

Why would I say that? I thought. But I had learned to cherish and allow my spontaneity, so I just went with it. Without a moment's pause, Wayne gave me a number where I could fax him what I had in mind. He didn't ask what I wanted to send him. As he had said to me during our conversation, God finds many different ways to speak to us.

Looking back, I'm very grateful that he trusted himself in contacting me and trusted me in sending him Anita Moorjani's NDE story, which had arrived in my inbox just the day before. I belong to a list of people who e-mail each other on spiritual topics, and one of the shared stories that day was a link to what Anita had written about her NDE. The excerpt that was included in the e-mail spoke of Anita's explanation of how all possibilities exist simultaneously. (If you would like to read the excerpt again, please refer to page 138 of this book.)

It is interesting to think how Spirit knew how to catch my eye. Because of my regression with John, the idea of simultaneous time was of great interest to me. Yet discussions on the existence of the afterlife are not novel for me, so if the excerpt had simply sounded like "an interesting NDE story," I would have most likely skipped it. Instead, I could tell that whatever Anita had written would be worth my time.

When my printer spat out 21 pages, I felt a sense of joy—so much to read! I knew I was in for a special treat. I grabbed a pen I love and sat down, ready to underline the gems of wisdom I knew I would find.

Reading Anita's story made me feel a magical sense that I had locked into the true vibration of my spirit. I felt like I had come across a magnificent piece of myself. Through regression I, like Anita, had come to know that all physical ailments begin on an energetic level. Even before reading her story, I believed that the body was capable of healing itself instantly if the dense film of negativity is removed.

And of course, Anita's story spoke to another topic that is very dear to my heart: the simultaneity of existence. Because all events unfold simultaneously in time, and all possibilities exist in the same one moment, we can weave through realities and create and experience what is most in harmony with our highest good. I loved everything about Anita's NDE experience and the information she shared.

Yet the moment Wayne and I hung up, that question crept up again: *Why do I feel so compelled to share Anita's story with him?* The only explanation I could think of was that it described so perfectly what I believed in and what I could offer him. By sending him Anita's story, I was saying to him, "I know you can be healed of the leukemia instantaneously. That possibility exists, and I can assist you in creating that reality." It would have taken a much longer conversation for me to say all that Anita had so simply and eloquently put into words through her story.

Now I see a second explanation for my spontaneous outburst: I understand that I am part of a process that sought to bring Anita's inspiring words to the entire planet. Wayne loved Anita's story so much that he forwarded it to his publisher, Hay House, and encouraged them to find the author and sign her up for a book—which they did! By following my enthusiasm and sharing my excitement, I served All That Is and All That Is served me. This is Oneness in action!

The timing of when Anita's story came to me was absolutely synchronous. Had it been sooner than the day it came to me, it would not have been at the forefront of my thoughts and I wouldn't have shared it with Wayne. Had it come later than that day, Anita and her profound words would most likely not be receiving the enormous recognition they're getting now. The synchronicity of this coming together so magically reminds us that everything happens at once, at the one same timeless moment. And because of that, the second we need whatever will serve us best is there to support us.

A few months and several conversations later, Wayne and I agreed to have a regression, so I flew out to Maui to meet with him. My trust that Wayne would heal was beyond praying or hoping—it was a deep and absolute knowingness. And indeed, Wayne's session was profoundly powerful in its healing.

I went back to the e-mail that brought Anita's story to me to find out who the sender was. Ozgian Zulchefil is an engineer who lives in Bucharest, Romania, and I did not know him before contacting him. I shared with him the awe-inspiring synchronicities that had been taking place and that he was part of. He was glad I had taken the time to tell him, even though he didn't remember where he'd found Anita's NDE story. He said that this served as a confirmation that we constantly affect one another by what we do and say, even if we're not aware of it. Therefore, he concluded, it is "important to have a really good positive attitude for every moment of your life, even if you don't see a reason for doing it in the first place." I couldn't help but smile.

Some time later I received another e-mail through the same list I subscribe to, suggesting that I watch an inspiring interview with a woman named Anita Moorjani, who had been miraculously healed of cancer following an NDE. A big surge of excitement went through me as I recalled how Wayne and I allowed for Anita's powerful words of love to uplift millions of people. Receiving that last e-mail confirmed that the circle had been completed energetically, and that Wayne and I had accomplished our task. At the same time, Anita's words assisted us in creating Wayne's healing.

After my session with Wayne, I returned to New York, my heart filled with gratitude. I was grateful to have assisted Wayne in healing from the leukemia, and to have helped release the emotional causes of it. I was thankful that by reaching out to him I had helped get Anita's profound story out to a wider audience. I was also thankful for the opportunity that Wayne and the Universe had given me to be who I knew myself to be in my heart—a regressionist.

As I walked into my apartment upon my return, my partner came to greet me at the door. He said hello and started asking about my trip, but then suddenly interrupted himself. He told me how different I looked and how different my energy felt. He was right. I had shifted into a new reality—I had shifted into a different Mira.

I knew that the time had come to live as the person I truly was. It was now or never. I quickly decided to no longer pursue my career in law and instead dedicate myself to the work that gave me such meaning and fulfillment. As if to let me know that I was on the right path, the Universe presented me with an invaluable gift: Wayne called to tell me that he'd be including the transcript of our session in his book *Wishes Fulfilled*.

Miracle after miracle was descending upon me. Since that time, my regression work has become my life. And my life has become a magical explosion of synchronicities supporting me on my path.

As if to encourage me again, the Universe recently presented me with yet another gift. Just a few days before submitting the manuscript for this book to my publisher, I received wonderful news: Brian Weiss was scheduled to appear on Oprah Winfrey's show *Super Soul Sunday*. And to acquaint the audience with Brian's great book *Miracles Happen*, he and Oprah had chosen to share the entire story of one of my past lives. Of all the stories told in *Miracles Happen*, they chose the one of the Russian doctor and her beloved American soldier. The news left me elated. I was grateful beyond words that my first regression experience would be featured on Oprah's website.

I felt as if I was doing nothing yet everything was being done *for* me. No amount of thinking, planning, or hoping could have given me the opportunity to submit stories for publication in

Brian and Amy's book, *Miracles Happen*. No amount of trying to figure things out would have resulted in my regressing Wayne, or in his including the transcript of our session in *Wishes Fulfilled*. No amount of action on my behalf could have landed the story of my first regression on Oprah.com. The only thing I had going for me was simple alignment. I was aligned with the energy of my highest good. I was aligned with the energy of service through the greatest expression of who I am. My energy was aligned with the energy of these people and the results they were looking to create.

Aligning myself involved no work. I simply allowed myself to follow what seemed interesting and exciting to me. I did not delve into the fascinating world of regression because I had the goal of one day having my work published in the books of such prominent authors as Wayne Dyer and Brian Weiss. I took all the steps I took simply because thinking, reading, and talking about regression were the most intriguing and fulfilling things in the world for me. I did not start out with a plan to make a career out of it. Had I been thinking rationally, I would never have spent so much time and money on something so far removed from my career as a lawyer—something that gave me only a sense of inner satisfaction. But therein lies the explanation for why my life has been graced with such miracles.

Letting Go of Doubt and Fear

Bashar, an entity channeled by Darryl Anka, teaches that excitement is the physical translation of the vibration your soul has chosen to create in life. The things that provoke those feelings in us are the things that are most *like* us. They reflect us in our highest representation. Joy points us toward whatever we are able to accomplish most effortlessly. At any given moment, Bashar encourages, we should act upon whatever opportunity excites us the most. When we act on what offers the highest levels of joy and excitement, we're saying that we have the faith to be our true selves and to act as our true selves.

Because we are always supported in who we are, whatever excites us expands our soul—joyfully and effortlessly. That said, expansion is not feasible unless we face and integrate whatever fears come up around our passions. Growing does not mean avoiding our fears or pretending that they're not there. The light does not push out the darkness—the light *penetrates* the darkness, infusing it with brightness. Growing means bringing your fears inside of you, seeing the beliefs that make them seem so potent, and then infusing them with new light and understanding.

Our greatest fear is where our greatest potential lies. Bashar tells us that we feel fear because the energy of our true self is being filtered through limiting beliefs. When those beliefs are examined, released, and replaced with supportive beliefs, we are able to expand more and more into our greatest self. Thus, the fear is simply a messenger who kindly tells us that we have taken on thoughts that do not belong to us. If we let those fears go, we will experience life in ever more ecstatic ways.

For me, the world of regression has always been very intriguing. Ever since that very first book I read when I was little, it has been a source of great curiosity and joy. Following the miraculous healing of my jaw, I gave my passion full rein. It seemed completely harmless at first. It was simply something that occupied my spare time, gave me a new way of seeing the world, and made for fascinating conversations. Because everything around the topic of regression was so gratifying, I allowed myself to continue to choose the greater and greater opportunities that were presenting themselves. The energy was building and forming a whole new life.

Meanwhile, in my legal career, I was representing companies whose securities were traded on the stock exchanges. My work was very closely tied to the developments on Wall Street. As a result, the financial crisis that was shaking the world in 2008 was also felt in my seemingly insulated world. The news that droves and droves of lawyers were losing their jobs every day created panic in everyone's heart, including mine. It felt as if the world were ending. The tension of the environment made me ask myself the obvious question: "If I lose my job, and can't get another one as a lawyer, what will I do?"

I remember sitting at my desk at work one day, staring at the wall in front of me, feeling a sense of urgency. I needed a plan, something to fall back on. I quickly took stock of all my skills and abilities. Because of the stress I felt, the examination I was conducting had the brutal honesty and clarity of Judgment Day.

The only skill I had to offer the world was my ability to regress people, catalyzing healing and transformation. I believe, in my desperate need for guidance, I had created an open channel to my Higher Self and was able to hear the answer very clearly. In that moment, regression was upgraded in my mind from a mere hobby to something that I could actually do for a living. Regression was already the channel through which I felt most like my true self. It made me feel alive and exuberantly happy. I was fully present and felt most connected to Source. I was accessing and being my true self: The prospect of being fulfilled and having meaningful work seemed so appealing, but the pleasure lasted only a second. A moment later I was choked by the death grip of anxiety. The recognition that I could do regressions for a living triggered massive bouts of fear.

My fears were all about money. I simply did not believe it was possible for healing work to pay the bills. Thankfully, I had time on my side. I was able to stay at my job for three more years, which gave me the time to work through the negative beliefs that were fueling my fears. Remember, your transformation will be as fast as you allow it to be. I took this long because this pace served me; it made me feel safe. I was very honest and thorough in examining my beliefs. I followed the principles I have shared in this book and combined them with tapping to release all of my limiting thoughts. I traced many of those thoughts to my childhood, and I realized that I had been hypnotized into an understanding of reality that had been passed on to me by my parents and to them from their parents.

I decided to honor my beliefs rather than fight them. If I invalidated them, I would invalidate everything I was and everything

I had created on the basis of those beliefs. By accepting their validity, I could gradually transform them into what I preferred to know as my new truth.

My Higher Self and my thinking mind were involved in a well-choreographed dance. My thinking mind was saying to my Higher Self, "I trust that in regression you are showing me something that could make me feel fulfilled each day. But I'm scared. I have so many financial obligations to provide for." My Higher Self responded, "I love you so much. I want the best for you, so I will keep you employed and give you all the time that you need to work through the limited thinking. You can trust me. I will keep you safe. I won't allow you to get hurt." To which my thinking mind said, "Thank you. I will do the work, but please give me signs that I am on the right path."

I slowly and diligently worked through my fears. Simultaneously, I allowed myself to step out more and more and present myself as a regressionist to the world. My Higher Self, true to its promise, offered me signs along the way that cheered and encouraged me.

By acting on my excitement, I reaffirmed my commitment to myself, my Higher Self, and the Universe. I was stepping into my greatest, happiest, most fulfilled self. I was grounding the energy in action. I was completing the circuit, and because of that Source was giving me more and more opportunities. I was acting on my excitement, and my bliss was showing me that regression could support me. The more regression supported me, the more I trusted it and the easier it was to take bigger actions that affirmed that joy. Bit by bit, I let go of the idea that my survival depended on lawyering. The light was slowly but surely penetrating the darkness, engulfing it in brightness.

○

We do not need to learn to trust; we need to learn not to doubt. As Bashar says, doubt is trusting 100 percent in a belief that is not in alignment with our true self. For example, if you are out of work and doubt that you'll ever find a well-paying job, you're putting all of your trust into the belief in scarcity—the belief that you're not enough.

If we are experiencing doubt, it's because we are trusting in something that is not in alignment with who we are. Our souls are able to create and experience physical reality because of the intense focus and trust they place on a particular set of circumstances. Through regression work, I have learned that in order to have a physical incarnation, we need to be in a state of total trust. It takes a great deal of trust to allow so much of our true nature and power to be forgotten and to place ourselves in a state of such limitation here on Earth. We already have within us the ability to fully and completely trust the Divine in the sojourn of each incarnation. Therefore, according to Bashar, we always trust. If we already have the mechanism of trust built in us, then all we have to do is direct it in order to experience the reality we desire.

Learning about this unusual perspective on trust gave me a sense of relief. I did not need to learn to trust. There was no hurdle to overcome. I already knew how to trust; in fact, I was trusting in every moment. What I needed to understand was why I would trust in thoughts of scarcity—specifically, the belief that I would not be financially supported for work that fully reflected my passion. And the answer was clear: The evil I knew was less scary than the evil I imagined.

The stress of my job, the long work hours, the expectation that I would be available to my clients at a moment's notice no matter the time of day or night, the absurdly tight deadlines, the exhaustion and lack of a personal life—all of these came as the evil I knew. I felt comfortable with it. I knew how to manage it. The thought that regression work could not support me financially was an evil far more frightening. Once I saw this, the question became, how would I allow myself to trust what I want to trust? I realized it was simply a matter of refocusing.

We hypnotize ourselves into believing certain things. We pick out a point of view—or a point of view is supplied to us—and we take it for granted without questioning it. Meantime, we exclude all opposing points of view. This is so automatic that we don't stop and ponder the different steps. I decided that I already knew how to hypnotize myself to believe in one assumption to the exclusion of all other possibilities. It worked so perfectly that I simply had to go through the same steps consciously, but this time instead focus my concentration on the things I preferred to believe in. The difference was subtle—I was simply aware and awake. But the results were profound.

I released the limiting beliefs about regression as a viable career. I also allowed myself to expand my understanding around being supported. I chose to really internalize that because God had created me and regression was the focus of my passion, the Universe wanted to see this joy expressed to its fullest in every moment. I knew that Source loved me unconditionally, and that it would support me in any way I wanted to know myself. It had supported me as someone who believed I could make money only as a lawyer. Why wouldn't it do the same if I redefined my preferences?

I now wanted to change the definition of who I was. I trusted that in its unconditional love and adoration of me, All That Is would support that creation, too. That is what unconditional love is —love and help without any restrictions or conditions. I chose to redefine what abundance meant for me. I chose to see that I am abundant not only in money but also in opportunities, friends, possibilities, and open hearts and minds.

I chose to trust the expansion of my being. I chose to trust the direction in which I was growing. I chose to trust that I would be supported for who I am. I chose to trust that I am loved for who I am. I chose to trust that the Universe was supporting me with its infinite abundance in every thought, in every idea, in every desire, and in every plan that I had. I decided to trust that this support was and is always appropriate and always right. I created a little mantra for myself: *I trust myself. I trust my life. I trust All That Is.*

It became my sacred incantation, and I am happy to share it with you. I invite you to write it on sticky notes and place them on your bathroom mirror, on your fridge, or on your computer at work. Commit this mantra to memory, and make it your own. Trust is really at the core of it all.

My focus was steady and clear. As time passed, miracles began unfolding all around me. Opportunities were arranging themselves in ways I could not have even conceived. I felt as if a current was carrying me along, and I was simply sitting in a boat and marveling at the scenery. I was trusting and living the wisdom of the Tao Te Ching, which says, "The Tao does nothing, yet leaves nothing undone."

Exercise: How to Find Your Purpose

"What is my life's purpose?"

This is the question I hear most often from my clients. It's very rare for a client to walk into my office completely clear on his or her mission in life. There's good reason why this question is paramount: It goes to the essence of who we are as beings. Translating creativity into action is expressing our essence—the reason we were created in the first place. Do you remember Serena's life where she described how and why souls are created? Source created you because your unique combination of energies fulfills a need—a void that was experienced in all of existence before you arrived. You were created with the purpose to be your own unique blend of colors.

As children we're often asked, "What are you going to be when you grow up?" We believe that we need to have a life-spanning career, a single title or goal that defines us. And when we don't see it, we become confused. We begin a frantic game of "Is this my career? What is my purpose? I don't know my purpose." We look for the answer externally, rather than internally.

Yet the answer is so simple. Your only purpose in life is to *be yourself*. That is why you were created—to be yourself fully and completely in every moment. Often this answer shocks people. "Surely it can't be that simple!" they say. They expect their "life's purpose" to be something big, something great, something worthy of their time. In truth, the greatest missions are accomplished step by step. A grand life is lived moment by moment. And what could be more worthy of your time than being yourself, fully and completely, in every moment?

The expression of this simple life purpose will be different for each of us, because each of us is different. To discover what the expression of your life purpose is, I offer you a process. Please set aside at least

20 minutes of quiet time. Ask yourself the questions that follow and write down the answers in your journal:

- What do you enjoy doing the most?

- What comes most easily to you?

- What are you good at?

- What do people praise you for?

- What makes you feel that time flies by?

- What do you get lost in?

Knowing the answer to these questions is the first step toward knowing your purpose. It gives you the general idea.

The second step is to ask yourself how you can anchor these skills in physical reality. Ask yourself, "How can I be of service to others through my abilities, through what gives me joy?" Meditate on this question and write down the answers that come to you. When you trust your impulses and honor your excitements, you will be led into action. Do not expect these actions to be "big"—they may or may not be. You don't need to know how these actions will create a career or a job. Each step will reveal the answer more and more. Step by step, a path will be created. All that matters is that you anchor your creative energies in physical reality by taking action. See what you wrote as a blueprint to follow in the days, months, and years to come.

The third and final step is to act on your joy. The key to living a purposeful life is to ask yourself, each moment, "Of all the options that I have available to me in this moment, what would give me the greatest joy, the greatest excitement, and the greatest fulfillment?" Then, choose that action. It really is that simple. Please take this question to heart; live from it. Let my story of how I followed my path encourage and inspire you. I never planned on my life being the way it is right now; I simply followed what felt exciting to me, step after step. Let go of the thought, *I don't know my purpose.* Even if you are only taking the tender first steps toward becoming who you are, make this your new affirmation: *I am living on purpose. In every moment I am choosing to be myself and acting on my excitement.*

Our purpose is to be who we are, and to act on what excites— all while serving others. So whenever this conversation arises, please share what you now know. Remind those around you that, by not being themselves, they are robbing existence of the very reason they were created. Teach the young ones around you, and encourage the adults to be more and more themselves in every moment. But most important, live your passion. Live your excitement. Because by being true to yourself, you are giving permission to those around you to live their purpose, too.

Can you imagine what a different world this would be if each and every one of us honored ourselves and God by just being who we are in every moment?

AFTERWORD

A LIFE OF GLORIOUS EXPANSION

Today, I continue to trust synchronicity to lead me where I need to go. My story is by no means complete. But it always warms my heart when people approach me and tell me how inspired they are by my journey—how I have allowed my path to take me from the law to past-life regression. If my story resonates with you, then it's been Divinely orchestrated that you would be reading these words. You too are in a place where you're seeking to create a life of glorious expansion. I am here to serve as an example, to assure you that each of us can be supported in doing what we love most. If you fully step into your power, you will experience a life of purpose and fulfillment that you may never have thought possible.

Allow for the lessons shared in this book to seep deeply into your consciousness. Think about them, and then apply them in your life. Do the exercises. Regress yourself and see the events of the past through the new perspectives presented here. Play with time. Allow for synchronicities, miracles, and magic. Forgive yourself and others. And most of all, *love*. We are all so good at loving others, but it's time to place an equal focus on loving ourselves. For when our own cup is full, we have so much more love, genuine and unconditional love, to offer others.

Keep this book with you. Carry it even when you're done reading it, as its energy will serve as a strong reminder of the true direction of your soul. Share the stories and the lessons with others. Be like me, and gift this book to every kindred spirit. Through your passion you can ignite sparks in others' hearts and minds. By teaching, you will understand even more. Trust yourself, trust your life, and trust the Universe. Most of all, know that you are loved and treasured *just as you are*. Source knew what it was doing when it created you. Source does not do pointless things.

I have allowed myself to grow into my true self, so I know that you can do it, too. You have attracted my story as an example because you hold within you that very same vibration. If you didn't hold the potential of your Highest Self and if it wasn't seeking to express itself, you wouldn't be able to perceive the expression of that potential in others. Because of that, I encourage you to trust your own expansion. Trust the direction in which your excitement is pulling you.

I have created a tool to assist you in your development. It is called *The Trust Meditation* and is focused on the ideas of self-love and trust. Please download this recording, free of charge, from my website: www.mirakelley.com/meditation-download. This meditation will allow you to effortlessly release your limiting beliefs and internalize how deserving, loved, and supported you are. It will guide you into trusting whatever you prefer, and aligning and creating your best life yet.

Appendix A in this book provides a transcript that you can use to regress yourself. You can either have a trusted friend read it to you or make a recording of your own voice reading the script. If you prefer, you can also use the guided regression that is part of my CD set, *Healing Through Past-Life Regression . . . and Beyond*. No matter which path you choose, regression will lead you into the fascinating world of experiences that magically transform people's lives. You will be able to revisit other lives you have lived. It will allow you to release emotional and physical traumas, and it will help you receive guidance from your Higher Self. After listening once, each subsequent time you listen you will go deeper and deeper. The depth of your trance will be more and more profound, and the potential of your explorations will be greater. Therefore, use it as often as your intuition guides you.

I would love to hear about your experiences, so please e-mail me: info@mirakelley.com and share your stories with me. I am truly blessed to be doing something that allows me to communicate with Spirit every day. I love being on the cutting edge of the expansion of our consciousness, and to be able to connect deeply with people, assist them with emotional and physical healing, and help them transform into their greater selves. Just the other day, a beautiful woman came all the way from Switzerland to see me. "Now I know why you love what you do so much," she said after the session was complete. She had just come out of the trance, and her face had that loving, relaxed look all my clients wake up with.

I send you oceans of love, and I thank you for allowing me to take you on this journey of adventure, transformation, and healing through past-life regression.

In Light, Love, and Oneness,

Mira Kelley

APPENDIX A
Past-Life Regression Transcript

What follows is a tool you can use to create your own regression experience. You can record yourself reading the transcript and play the recording to yourself, or you can have a trusted friend read it for you. Whatever you decide, the key is to read the transcript slowly, with a gentle and soft voice. Be sure to allow for a pause between the paragraphs. If a longer pause is needed, I have indicated that in brackets at the end of the paragraph. If you're savvy with technology, you can add relaxing music you enjoy as a background to the recording of your voice. If not, you can play the music on a separate device. Music is not a requirement, though—it's simply an opportunity for you to enjoy the process even more.

Do the regression lying down or sitting in a comfortable chair. I suggest that you do the regression at a time of day when you're fresh and relaxed, as opposed to before bedtime when you're tired and likely to drift off. (For more information on what you can expect during your experience, please see Appendix B.) Most important, trust yourself and trust that you will be given exactly what will serve your highest good.

The regression will take approximately 30 minutes. Afterward, give yourself plenty of time to process what you've experienced. Journal about anything that came up, including feelings, thoughts, images, and realizations. You may also choose to meditate or go for a walk to reflect on the life you connected to.

Here is the regression transcript:

Allow your eyes to gently close.

Take a deep breath in and slowly let it out.

Allow yourself to begin to relax.

Allow yourself to begin to float.

As you take your next breath in, see or feel or imagine the Divine light of Source surrounding you.

See or feel or imagine how this white light is beginning to slowly sink into your feet.

This beautiful white light is warming and relaxing the muscles of your feet.

Feel this light making its way from your feet all the way up your legs.

Feel the light warming you.

Feel your feet and legs relaxing.

The light is soothing and relaxing the muscles of your calves, relaxing your knees.

Feel the light moving up through and relaxing the bones and muscles of your legs.

See the energy moving through the hip muscles and the hipbones, continuing up gently and easily.

Allow the light to relax the muscles of your abdomen.

Feel it soothing and relaxing your stomach.

Feel or see the light slowly and gently rising in your chest, allowing for your breath to be deep and even.

With your next breath in, feel how light and open and expanded your chest is.

You are becoming more and more relaxed.

Now feel or see or imagine the white light surrounding your heart . . . infusing your heart.

Feel the energy of your heart being purified.

And now with every next beat of your heart, your heart is spreading these feeling of tranquility and peace . . . this Divine white light . . . through the arteries, through the veins to every organ, to every tissue, to every cell of your body.

And you are feeling more and more deeply relaxed.

See or feel the light moving up your fingertips. Soothing and relaxing the muscles of your hands. Allowing your hands to rest easily.

Feel the white light climbing up your elbows, all the way up to your shoulders.

See or imagine the white light moving from your hips to your back, soothing and relaxing the muscles of your lower back, gently climbing up your spine.

Just for this little while, you can set aside all the troubles of the world that you carry on your shoulders. There is enough time for them later.

Feel the muscles of your shoulders relaxing and all the tension stored there releasing.

Now the light that is rising up your arms is blending with the white light that is rising in your chest and up your back.

And you are becoming more and more deeply relaxed.

Feel and see the white light climbing up your neck, soothing and relaxing the muscles of your neck and inside your throat.

Feel the white light moving up to your head and to your face.

Allow your jaw to relax. Allow your lips to relax. Allow your tongue to relax.

Feel all of the muscles of your face . . . the skin on your face . . . your scalp . . . and even your ears relax.

Allow your eyes to relax.

Feel the white light sinking gently into your brain.

In your imagination now see the symbol for infinity, the number 8 tilted on its side.

Now imagine and trace with your mind how the light moves from one side of the brain to the other . . . circling around the hemispheres . . . tracing the symbol for infinity . . . following the path of infinity.

Back and forth . . . back and forth . . . back and forth from one side of the brain to the other.

By doing this, you are allowing for the two brain halves to harmonize . . . you are allowing for your body and for your mind to synchronize . . . and you are allowing for your mind to synchronize with your Higher Self.

Feel your mind, your mentality, your thoughts beginning to relax.

All of your fears, all of your worries, all of your doubts are relaxing. They are all blending and melting into the relaxation of your body. You feel peaceful and calm . . . and deeply relaxed.

Between the two brain halves there is a small gland called the pineal gland. The pineal gland allows us to connect with other dimension, with other frequencies . . . with other lifetimes.

Imagine now the white light gently massaging the pineal gland so that it naturally and easily produces DMT (dimethyltryptamine, also known as the spirit molecule) to assist us in the explorations we are doing today.

Feel or see or imagine the white light surrounding you so that you are in a cocoon of white light . . . a bubble of white light.

You are protected. You are safe. You feel it and you know it. *[long pause]*

You are now open. You are now relaxed. You are now willing to be balanced. You are now willing to be healed. You are now willing to be transformed. You are now willing to be unconditionally loved.

In your mind now invite the angels to come and join us and support us with their love, light, and healing energy. *[long pause]*

As you remain in the cocoon of white light, feel or see or imagine four angels joining you. Any way, shape, or form you imagine them or see them is perfect.

See how the angels arrange themselves around you. One is on your head. One is at your feet. And one on each side of your body.

Feel how their energy gently connects with your energy . . . and how they slowly and easily lift the bubble of white light that you are in.

Allow yourself to relax in their arms. Allow yourself to float . . . feeling safe and protected.

The angels are lifting you higher and higher . . . higher and higher.

The angels can carry you through time and space, in any direction of time and space.

I am asking the angels now to move and carry you through time and space to another time, to another place where there is something important for you to learn and understand . . . something that will help you in the very best way.

The angels are carrying you.

Drifting and floating . . . drifting and floating through time and space.

You are feeling protected and safe . . . comfortable and relaxed.

The angels know the way. They are taking you to a place and time where there is something important for you to learn and understand.

Drifting and floating . . . drifting and floating through time and space . . .

And now the angels are stopping. They are bringing the bubble of white light that you are in back down, down, down to the surface.

The bubble of light is on the surface now.

I am going to count from 3 to 1, and when I reach 1, you will be on the other side of the bubble.

3 . . . move through the white light;

2 . . . moving through the light;

1 . . . be on the other side of it now.

You are in another place, another time.

Look around you.

Engage all of your senses.

What are the first things that you see around you?

What are the first feelings or impressions that you have?

Look down at your feet. Do you have anything on your feet?

Look at your legs and your torso. Are you wearing any clothes? If you have clothes on, what do they look like? *[long pause]*

Stretch your hands in front of you and look at them. Are you holding anything? *[long pause]*

Do you have any decorations anywhere on your body?

Are you a man or a woman?

How old are you?

What do you look like?

Is it daytime or nighttime?

Are there any others with you? *[long pause]*

Explore the important events in this life. *[long pause]*

If anything makes you feel uncomfortable, rise above the scene and continue to observe from above. You can continue to watch from a distance knowing that you are safe and protected. *[long pause]*

You can go backward and forward in time to learn more and allow the story of the life to develop fully. *[long pause]*

Do you recognize any of the people as people you now know? *[long pause]*

Now go to the last day of your life and experience how your spirit leaves the body without any pain or struggle. *[long pause]*

What lessons did you learn in this life? *[long pause]*

How is this experience connected to your present life? *[long pause]*

What is important for you to know about your present life? *[long pause]*

Drift away from these scenes now . . . drift away . . . float away.

Allow yourself to drift away from these scenes.

Information will continue to be provided to you by your Higher Self, your guides, and your angels in your dreams and in your waking moments as intuition, signs, and inspired thoughts. Your dreams will be more vivid over the next few nights, and you will remember them more clearly than ever.

Now it is time to return back to your present life. You will remember everything you experienced very clearly. Anytime you listen to this recording and do a regression, you will always receive guidance, healing, and help from your angels. And it will always be a very transformative, healing, and pleasant experience.

Now I will count from 5 to 1. On the count of 1, you will be awake and refreshed and you will feel wonderful.

5 . . . begin to come up;

4 . . . orient yourself to the present moment and to the present time;

3 . . . begin to awake now; you feel rested and refreshed;

2 . . . you can stretch your arms and legs;

1 . . . open your eyes. You are wide awake and you feel wonderful: loved, rested, and replenished.

APPENDIX B

Frequently Asked Questions about Past-Life Regression

Here I would like to answer some of the most frequently asked questions I receive on the subject of past-life regression and the sessions I offer.

Q. Can I get stuck in a past life?

A. After listening to me describe what our session will be like, people often ask whether they might get stuck in another life and never return. I assure them that they are absolutely safe. Regression is experienced the way you experience a memory— be it a moment from your childhood or what you had for dinner last night. When you place your focus on a particular moment, the images, thoughts, feelings, and details that comprise it will pop into your mind. But in the same way that you cannot get stuck in a memory, you also cannot get stuck in a past life.

Q. What if I experience something scary?

A. People often wonder, *What if I experience something terrifying and it messes me up even more than I already am?* I assure my clients that regression is not like going to the movies to see a horror film—it is not done for the purpose of scaring you out of your mind for no reason! Regressions are done with the intention of healing, of revealing what will serve your highest good. Even if you experience something emotional, it will not seem frightening to you. For example, to some it may seem upsetting to hear me talk about my life as the slave with the metal collar around my neck. You may hope you don't experience that kind of horror. Yet for me, there was nothing scary about that life. There were plenty of emotions—sadness, anger, and rivers of tears. But those were cathartic and healing. The lives where there were challenges are *your* lives. They are already part of your energy vibration. They will not seem foreign or disturbing when you relive them, because they are yours. Subconsciously, you are already familiar with them; you are already connected with them.

I also want to assure you that your Higher Self, angels, and guides are watching over you and will not give you an experience you cannot handle. An example of that is my first regression as a child, when I saw the life of the Russian spy. When I revisited that life as an adult, I saw details that had not shown up the first time I'd seen it. These were details that were painful and could have affected my psyche as a young girl. But I was guided and protected; I was given only as much as I could handle. I simply ask my clients to know that they are guided and protected, and to trust—to trust both themselves and Source.

Q. Will I be hypnotized?

A. This question is often linked with the fear of being controlled—forced to do something against our will through mind manipulation. Regression does use hypnosis, but it is very, very different from the common perception we have of it. Most people have seen "hypnosis" performed onstage, for the purpose of entertainment. Stage hypnosis is based on an unspoken contract that is agreed upon when the audience volunteers walk onstage. The hypnotist shows up expecting his or her commands to be taken and obeyed. The person who chooses to be the show's guinea pig agrees that he or she will follow the instructions received. This is very important to understand, because you cannot be controlled unless you agree to it.

I assure my clients that they will remain in complete control throughout our session together. If something feels uncomfortable or becomes emotional, they can always open their eyes, get up, and walk away. If such an impulse should arise, my preference is for clients to stay in the experience and convey it to me, so that I can become a better guide. But the choice is theirs. During a regression, each of us is always in complete control.

Hypnosis starts with feeling safe, allowing yourself to become relaxed and focusing your attention on the images and emotions that rise within. In reality, it is nothing more than an altered brain-wave state—a state of deep relaxation and creativity. These are typical brain states for all of us, so most of my clients aren't even aware that they're being "hypnotized." Let me explain how it works.

In normal waking consciousness, your brain operates in beta brain waves. When you begin to relax, your brain easily moves from a beta-wave state to an alpha-wave state. With my guidance, clients move even deeper—from alpha to theta. Theta is the state of being aware but drowsy. Everyone experiences this state each night before falling asleep and again in the morning before waking up. Theta is the border state between consciousness and unconsciousness. It is a state where profound learning, healing, and growth take place.

However, instead of moving deeper into theta, some clients' brains move from alpha up into gamma—operating at an even higher frequency than beta. In this state, you have a heightened sense of perception and consciousness, and you experience Oneness with all, a sense of bliss, and an innate understanding of the nature of existence.

During our time together, with my guidance, clients remain in either a theta or gamma state, allowing for our powerful work to take place. This is a state that a person's body and mind are very familiar with; to them, it feels natural and easy. Because these are familiar states, and because the brain seamlessly shifts between states, people assume that nothing is happening to them, that they are not being hypnotized.

Another reason people may not recognize that they are being hypnotized is that they assume hypnosis means they will be unconscious. Indeed, many of the people I see believe that for past-life regression to work, they should not be consciously aware. They imagine I will be having a session with an unconscious part of them, so that when they wake up, they have no memories of what has happened. Now truth be told, this has happened—but it is extremely rare. With most clients, the conscious mind is present through the entire experience. Clients know that they are lying on the sofa and I am sitting on a chair nearby. Simultaneously, they are allowing all sorts of experiences to arise in their head and are reporting them to me.

I believe that there is a very good reason why people are conscious during their regressions. Times have changed. Rigid religious beliefs do not have the same stronghold on people's lives as they did centuries ago. More and more people are becoming comfortable with their own connection to God, and with their ability to be guided directly by the Divine. Because religious constraints are not as limiting to us, we believe it's possible to have a direct connection and experience of Source and our own divinity. Thus, there is no reason for a part of us to hide what we learn about ourselves from the other parts of us. Not only can we handle our learning, but we are also consciously *seeking* that kind of understanding. We pursue our own enlightenment. We consume information and take actions that allow us to become whole, to integrate all parts of ourselves. There is no need for the mind to suppress what it has relived through a regression. The mind becomes part of the process. By witnessing everything, the mind is free to process it all and find the most beneficial ways to apply the information.

Because clients are conscious throughout the entire session, however, it is very easy for the mind to judge and put a stop to the experience. Clients are in full control; they can easily say, "This makes no sense" or "This is not how I've read about that era in history books."

For this reason, I ask my clients to suspend their judgments and simply allow for the mind to be intrigued and amused by what pops up. They will have all the time in the world following our session to analyze and make sense of what they have seen.

Q. How do I actually connect with my past lives?

A. Once I answer all questions my clients have, we begin the experiential portion of the session. The regression process itself is very simple and gentle. I have clients lie down, in the most comfortable position possible. I begin by guiding them into a deep state of relaxation. By closing their eyes and tuning within, they naturally decrease the levels of input from their five senses—sight, smell, touch, taste, and hearing. By relaxing the body, they are able to concentrate within, to the exclusion of other data.

The altered brain-wave states mentioned previously allow our consciousness and awareness to expand. This is how we are able to tune in to other lives we have lived. The information, guidance, and healing other lives provide is always present and available for us to connect with. With my guidance, clients merge their consciousness with those other lives.

Clients are able to intuitively identify who they are, and the images, sounds, and smells begin to flow. I ask clients to trust the first impressions, thoughts, and feelings that come to them. I also ask that they don't judge anything, even if it doesn't make sense. Everything is Divinely orchestrated. Things always come together perfectly and make sense at the end of the regression.

Q. Will I be imagining what I'm seeing?

A. People often wonder, *What if I'm only imagining my other lives?* To which I answer, there is no problem. Often imagination is the bridge that leads us into the story of a past life.

Recently, I did a session with a woman named Debbie. After I guided her into relaxation, I asked her what she felt, saw, or experienced.

"Nothing," she said.

"If you were to imagine something, what would it be?" I asked.

"A cave." What an interesting choice! It is unlikely that either you or I would have imagined a cave, if someone were to ask us that question.

"If you were to imagine something else, what would it be?" I asked Debbie. "People in the cave," she said. This was even more interesting! She described the people not as Neanderthals, as you might think, but as a Native American tribe. They were in the cave taking shelter from a storm. As she was saying this, Debbie became very emotional. She frantically began looking for her son among the people, but he was not there. She knew he was still out there, and she feared she had lost him.

The life began with a moment of imagination, yet it quickly turned into something personal and very meaningful for Debbie. When she came to see me, she was considering separating from her husband, but she was paralyzed with an irrational fear that she would lose custody of their little boy. This moment of allowing her imagination to run free let the connection with the past life be known. She understood that what seemed like an irrational fear actually had its root in a parallel life.

Imagination does not mean that you're connecting with something unreal. In the realm of Spirit, the past, present, and future all exist simultaneously. All things that have ever existed and will ever exist are present in the same "now" moment. You and I are unable to imagine what does not exist. If you try, you will only be able to think of a physical representation of nonexistence. I usually imagine nonexistence as a black void separated by a wall from everything that exists. That image, itself, is existence. Therefore, anything we can imagine already exists in some form or another —in one dimension of existence or another. Imagining is the act of connecting with available information.

Imagination is actively used as a psychotherapeutic method. Carl Jung and many other psychologists have theorized that the images in our fantasies may stem from deeper emotional traumas and unresolved conflicts from our pasts. Psychotherapists often help their clients by using imagination to process their repressed negative emotions and to find solutions to their challenges. Even if what is seen during a regression is "imagined," psychologists would still find value in it because the visions come from the person's subconscious mind. The subconscious knows how to heal us. Therefore, even if the images experienced during a regression are imagined, they still have tremendous therapeutic value.

I encourage clients to imagine freely, knowing that they are allowing the energy to flow and the Higher Self to guide them toward a life that will serve their highest good. After just a few moments of imagining, the story always—*always*—changes, and the client shifts into vivid emotional and healing experiences. As such, the first moments of imagination are simply a tool that gives the client permission to allow information to move through.

Q. What will happen during my regression?

A. Every session is unique. Each reflects the particular circumstances and needs of the person being regressed. Some people experience a life from birth through death—what we would think of as a "normal" human life. Other clients experience themselves as different life forms, such as dinosaurs, monkeys, flowers, and frogs. In other lives people are entities who live on other planets or on spaceships. And then there are those mystical experiences where people meet with their angels or guides, see how souls are created, or experience what the primal Source of all is like.

In addition, the way people experience regression is very different. Some see movies flowing in their minds, rich with details. When these sessions happen, I jokingly think to myself, *We need a whole lifetime just to revisit this one!* Then there are the experiences where a person sees a brief flash of an image that is coupled with emotions and a sense of knowing of what the story is. For others, the regressions are entirely an emotional experience, where the stories are known through feelings. And of course there are the sessions where clients hear or "touch" things and describe them to me.

In other words, there is no "right" way for past or future lives to be revisited. Whether you are working with me or alone with a recorded regression, I assure you that no matter how the experiences come up for you, you're doing everything right. Just trust and allow.

Q. What is the "Higher Self"?

A. After people reconnect with as many other lifetimes as necessary and are still in a deep state of trance, I ask that they connect with their Higher Self. This is what I like to refer to that bigger, wiser, and unconditionally loving part of our soul as. For me, the Higher Self holds the template of our greatest potential. It represents the greatest possible manifestation of certain themes and goals the soul would like to explore in a life. It is the highest possible achievement our soul would like to embody.

Each one of us has a Higher Self. Our Higher Self is part of us —it's the vibration of our true self. When I talk with a client's Higher Self, the client connects with the Higher Self's frequency and accesses its clarity of understanding. By doing so, the client *becomes* that vibration. This is one of the reasons why my regression sessions are so transformative and profound.

During my conversation with the Higher Self, I seek answers to the questions the person and I discussed before our session began. I also ask that the Higher Self heal any physical symptoms the person experiences and their emotional causes. Just as with revisiting the other lives, there is no one way to experience the connection with the Higher Self. Each person's experience is unique. I always encourage people to trust and allow whatever comes to be spoken. From that place of expanded awareness, some clients simply know the answers and give them to me. Others feel as if an energy surrounds them and they are pulling the answers from this energy. Still others report that it's as if someone else is speaking *through* them. None of these is any more beneficial than the others. Each of us has a different way of accessing guidance from our Higher Self.

When the work is done, I bring the person out of the trance. To him or her it frequently seems that the trance lasted only a few brief moments. In fact, usually a few hours have passed. The client's perception of time is distorted because at such deep levels of trance the person connects with other dimensions of existence and detaches from keeping up with time in this reality.

Q. What does the regressionist see during the session?

A. When people come into my office, I know that they're going to have an experience. However, I never know *what* experience they will have! In the beginning, when they share about their life, I am like a blank canvas. I simply listen, ask questions, and take notes. By suspending all judgment and simply understanding, I allow for our energies to blend. Once the regression is under way, something unusual happens within me. I am frequently able to see the images and hear information about what clients are experiencing, often seeing the entirety of the life they're describing before the images even come to them. This allows me to be an even better regressionist, because I'm not leading them blindly. Every time it happens, it serves as a reminder that we are all one—that we are all connected to the same one universal stream of information. It also tells me that, because there is no past or future, in a parallel timeline the session has already happened. The client has already had the experiences that, in linear time, are still to come.

It is as if I am blending my consciousness with the client's, and together we are traveling through time and space. Because we are all part of the same one primary consciousness, the moment we pan out from the intense association with one single aspect of the All—meaning our own body and personality—and place our attention on something outside of ourselves, we immediately become it. Therefore, when I perceive what clients experience, my consciousness may be merging with theirs into the consciousness of the One and traveling with them to other places and other times.

Q. Do you have any other advice to guide me when I do your guided regression?

A. There are a couple more things I would like to suggest. If you have pets in the house, leave them in another room behind a closed door. Pets are naturally attracted to soothing energy, so as the regression progresses and you begin to relax, they will want to be part of it. Rather than having them startle you and disrupt the experience, close the door. This ensures that you won't be interrupted.

The second thing I would like to suggest is that you pay attention to your dreams in the days that follow the regression. People often connect with other lives in their dreams. This is particularly the case after people have consciously sought to connect with their counterparts. Before you go to bed, give yourself this simple suggestion: *I will remember my dreams when I wake up in the morning.* Then in the morning, as soon as you become aware that you are awake, continue to lie in bed with your eyes closed and go over your dreams. The more you practice this, the easier it will become.

I recently did a radio-show interview, and in preparation for our conversation, the host had listened to the guided regression on my CD set. As the regression began, she experienced something unexpected that startled her. She pulled herself out of the vision and stopped it. That night she woke up from a dream that was connected to the vision in the regression and gave her very specific information on how to proceed forward with her creative work and her life's purpose.

I love this story because it is such a great example of how, when we consciously open up to guidance, the information we need always finds its way to us.

FURTHER RESOURCES

You can download my free 20-minute guided meditation focused on self-love and trust called *The Trust Meditation* at: www.mirakelley.com/meditation-download.

If you prefer for me to guide you into a past-life regression, please get a copy of my CD set, *Healing Through Past-Life Regression . . . and Beyond.* It has a guided past-life regression and a guided meditation. You can download it or get a physical copy at: www.MiraKelley.com or www.HayHouse.com.

If you would like to have a personal regression session with me, please e-mail me: info@mirakelley.com.

If you would like to join me for a past-life regression workshop or a retreat, please visit www.MiraKelley.com/events.

You can read about my profound past-life regression with Dr. Wayne W. Dyer in his book *Wishes Fulfilled.*

In *Miracles Happen* by Brian Weiss and Amy Weiss, you can read three regression stories I have contributed—two of my own and one client's story.

Please join a Facebook community of like-minded people where you can learn more about past-life regression, share your own past lives, and share your reactions to this book. The name of the group is *Past-Life Regression,* and you can find it at: www.facebook.com/groups/PastLifeRegression.

ACKNOWLEDGMENTS

To my physical teachers, Brian L. Weiss and Dolores Cannon: Thank you for creating the path that I now walk on. I greatly admire and appreciate your pioneering work. Thank you for awakening me to my true self, and for teaching me the tools to assist others in their transformation and healing.

To my nonphysical teachers, Seth and Bashar, and their human counterparts, Jane Roberts and Darryl Anka: Your energy has always been there to guide me, and your words have always been there to awaken me to the remembrance of my true essence. Thank you.

To John: Looking back now I see that our memorable session was Divinely orchestrated. It was meant to serve a purpose much larger than we could have imagined. Neither you nor I knew that when we met, our session would become something so important for both of us and for the world. For me it was the seed that became the impetus for writing this book. For you it became the way to remind yourself of your own path and to fulfill your purpose of teaching people understanding—something you are accomplishing through your sharing in this book. I am so grateful for your friendship, John. Thank you a million times for the gifts you brought into my life.

To all my clients whose stories I have shared here: Meeting you and being able to witness the magnificent spirits that you are has been a cherished blessing. I know your stories will touch the hearts of those who read this book, just as they did mine. Thank you for assisting me in the creation of this book and allowing me to see Source manifesting itself through the wondrous beings each of you are.

To Evan Kelley: Thank you for allowing me to regress you all these countless times. Your love and support for my interest in regression has allowed me to grow into the person I am today. You always believed in me, even when I could not see. Thank you for being there for me.

To Dr. Wayne W. Dyer: Thank you for trusting your inner guidance and allowing me and past-life regression to come into your life to help transform it. Words cannot express how grateful I am for your love and avid support. Thank you for believing in me and my work. Thank you! Thank you! Thank you!

To Reid Tracy: Thank you for your vision for my book and for your support of my work. You knew the value of this book before I could even dare to dream.

To Shannon Littrell: I could not ask for a better editor! Thank you for all you have done for me, both on this book and my CD set, *Healing Through Past-Life Regression . . . and Beyond*.

To Kelly Notaras: I love how when pronounced, my last name sounds like your first name. Where I end you begin. Thank you for blending your comments and thoughtful input on the manuscript so perfectly with my voice to create together a book that I believe will assist many people.

To Tamra Edgar: Thank you for all your help, love, and support. Our energies and vision are so perfectly aligned that I am sure we have been together in other lifetimes working side by side.

To Liliana Angelova Paslieva: I am blessed to have you, most amazing woman, as my mom. You have an infinite capacity for love and patience. Your spirit is joyful and kind. You teach me selflessness and devotion. You have always been very interested in everything about me—everything I have to say, every friend, every relationship, every school or career choice, every twist and turn in my life, and now the discoveries of my regression work. You have always believed in me and have encouraged me to have faith in myself. You have always been my "believing eyes," fully supporting my dreams and offering words of wisdom when I need it. No one can make things right the way you can. You know how to encourage me to be a better person and to celebrate the good things about me. You are my best friend, my inspiration, and my companion on the spiritual path. Your Divine energy always nurtures me and nourishes me. Mame, allow me to express my gratitude for all that you are and all that you have done for me by dedicating this book to you.

ABOUT THE AUTHOR

Mira Kelley grew up in Bulgaria, where at the age of 13 she had a powerful regression experience. With great courage and trust in her heart, Mira followed her intuition and came to the United States to go to college. Following her graduation from law school, Mira practiced as a corporate and securities attorney at a large firm in New York City. A painful physical condition led her to rediscover the instantaneous emotional and physical healing available through regression, and now she assists people in transforming their own lives in this way. Stories from Mira's sessions are included in *Wishes Fulfilled* by Dr. Wayne W. Dyer and *Miracles Happen* by Brian L. Weiss, M.D.; they have also been featured on Oprah.com.

Website: www.mirakelley.com

○○○

We hope you enjoyed this Hay House book. If you'd like to receive our online catalog featuring additional information on Hay House books and products, or if you'd like to find out more about the Hay Foundation, please contact:

Hay House, Inc., P.O. Box 5100, Carlsbad, CA 92018-5100
(760) 431-7695 or (800) 654-5126
(760) 431-6948 (fax) or (800) 650-5115 (fax)
www.hayhouse.com® • www.hayfoundation.org

Published and distributed in Australia by: Hay House Australia Pty. Ltd., 18/36 Ralph St., Alexandria NSW 2015 • *Phone:* 612-9669-4299 • *Fax:* 612-9669-4144 www.hayhouse.com.au

Published and distributed in the United Kingdom by: Hay House UK, Ltd., Astley House, 33 Notting Hill Gate, London W11 3JQ • *Phone:* 44-20-3675-2450 *Fax:* 44-20-3675-2451 • www.hayhouse.co.uk

Published and distributed in the Republic of South Africa by: Hay House SA (Pty), Ltd., P.O. Box 990, Witkoppen 2068 • *Phone/Fax:* 27-11-467-8904 www.hayhouse.co.za

Published in India by: Hay House Publishers India, Muskaan Complex, Plot No. 3, B-2, Vasant Kunj, New Delhi 110 070 • *Phone:* 91-11-4176-1620 *Fax:* 91-11-4176-1630 • www.hayhouse.co.in

Distributed in Canada by: Raincoast Books, 2440 Viking Way, Richmond, B.C. V6V 1N2 • *Phone:* 1-800-663-5714 • *Fax:* 1-800-565-3770 • www.raincoast.com

Take Your Soul on a Vacation

Visit www.HealYourLife.com® to regroup, recharge, and reconnect with your own magnificence. Featuring blogs, mind-body-spirit news, and life-changing wisdom from Louise Hay and friends.

Visit www.HealYourLife.com today!